Entrepreneurship for Creative Scientists

Entrepreneurship for Creative Scientists

Dawood Parker
Melys Diagnostics Ltd, UK

Surya Raghu
Advanced Fluidics LLC, USA

Richard Brooks
FD Solutions Ltd, UK

IOP Publishing, Bristol, UK

ISBN   978-0-7503-1146-5 (ebook)
ISBN   978-0-7503-1147-2 (print)
ISBN   978-0-7503-1148-9 (mobi)

DOI   10.1088/978-0-7503-1146-5

Version: 20180501

IOP Expanding Physics
ISSN 2053-2563 (online)
ISSN 2054-7315 (print)

British Library Cataloguing-in-Publication Data: A catalogue record for this book is available from the British Library.

Published by IOP Publishing, wholly owned by The Institute of Physics, London

IOP Publishing, Temple Circus, Temple Way, Bristol, BS1 6HG, UK

US Office: IOP Publishing, Inc., 190 North Independence Mall West, Suite 601, Philadelphia, PA 19106, USA

This book is dedicated to the many students and other delegates around the world who attended our workshops on 'Entrepreneurship for Scientists and Engineers'.
We are very grateful for the many contributions made during discussions at these workshops which have added significantly to this book.

Contents

Preface   viii

Acknowledgements   ix

Author biographies   x

1   Scientists as entrepreneurs   1-1

2   Selling your invention—options 1 and 2   2-1

3   Selling your invention—options 3 and 4   3-1

4   A start-up—formalities   4-1

5   Patenting your invention   5-1

6   Writing a business plan   6-1

7   A business plan   7-1

8   Raising funds   8-1

9   Managing a start-up   9-1

10   In conclusion   10-1

Appendix   A-1

Preface

This book sets out to clarify for scientists and engineers the steps that are necessary to take an idea along the path to commercialization and possible success. The difference between a scientist and an entrepreneur is discussed and the consequence to an enterprise of misunderstanding this difference. The book deals essentially with businesses started by scientists and based on innovation. The concept of patent protection is explained as is the process of applying for a patent. Finance and fund-raising are extensively dealt with, topics approached by scientists with little enthusiasm.

The book takes the reader through the need for a business plan and gives examples of how such a plan might look. The plan is meant, among other things, to clarify the strategy of the business and to determine the money that the company will need, when, and how often. Fund-raising is discussed at length in the book with particular attention focussed on the technique of 'pitching' for funds. Perhaps to the surprise of creative scientists, it is the management team and the personality of the entrepreneur that will count for much more with investors than the brilliant idea!

Much emphasis is put on the need for an inspiring and experienced management team for start-up companies. Here the founder scientist of the company often has to settle for appointing an entrepreneur as his/her boss—sometimes a decision that is unnecessarily delayed. Then there are the customers. The book points out, unsurprisingly, that they are the most important component for a successful business. The importance of a credible market survey is stressed.

The book deals with scientists who start companies as the entrepreneur or with an entrepreneur as the CEO and who take an invention all the way through to product launch. It also deals with those scientists who, acting as entrepreneurs, take a shorter route to commercialization by selling their intellectual property, generally to an established company, while retaining their full-time employment in academia or elsewhere.

Acknowledgements

We would like to give our sincere thanks to everyone who has helped with the writing of this book.

In particular, we would like to thank Yumiko Hamano for invaluable help on the complex subject of patents, and to Gareth Williams of Skyscanner for very useful advice drawn from running an especially successful start-up. Also, thanks to David Wooldridge of the Welsh Government Business Innovation Programme for his very thoughtful comments on the intellectual property sections of this book, and to Amir Shadmand, CEO and Co-founder of Supenta, for his advice on writing a business plan.

This book would not have been written without the decision of the Institute of Physics UK to run entrepreneurship workshops for scientists and engineers around the world. We would like to thank the speakers and the many delegates for their enthusiastic contributions to the workshops which have found their way into the contents of this book.

Author biographies

Dawood Parker

Dawood Parker read Physics and Mathematics at the University of Cape Town and obtained his PhD in Physics at Southampton University. He was a lecturer in Medical Physics in University College, London where he founded and was appointed Director of the Medical Instrumentation Unit, a research group which collaborated with and was supported by industry. He played a significant role in the development of continuous invasive and non-invasive techniques used in the care and management of pre-term infants. In 1978 he spent a year as a consultant at Critikon Inc, Irvine, California, (a Johnson and Johnson company), where he was involved in the research, development and production of sensors for patient monitoring.

He became a Fellow of the Institute of Physics in 1985. In 1986 he was awarded a personal chair in Physics in the University of Wales, Swansea, where he was the Director of the Biomedical Sensors Unit.

From 1984 to 1989 he was Consultant Director of Research and Development, Novametrix Medical Systems Inc., Wallingford, Connecticut. He has been a consultant to a number of major pharmaceutical companies.

In the last few years he has been involved in university–industry collaboration and has initiated a number of start-up companies which have resulted in the launch of successful patient monitoring instrumentation. Three of his start-up companies were acquired by major international pharmaceutical companies. He is currently Managing Director of Melys AFS Ltd and Melys Diagnostics Ltd, both of which are involved in the development of non-invasive patient monitoring systems.

He has published many scientific papers and holds a number of patents. He was awarded the MBE in 2013.

Dr Surya Raghu

Dr Surya Raghu received his PhD degree in mechanical engineering from Yale University in 1987. He was a post-doctoral fellow at Yale, a Humboldt Scholar at the Technical University of Berlin, Germany, Assistant Professor at SUNY, Stony Brook, visiting scientist at NIST and AFOSR Laboratories, and R&D Team Leader at Bowles Fluidics Corporation and has been the founder-president of Advanced Fluidics LLC since 2001.

Dr Raghu is currently involved in the development of products related to physiological monitoring, DNA testing, wireless corrosion sensors, aerodynamic flow control and spray technology. These products are being developed as joint collaborations with SMEs in the UK and the US. He has been awarded 11 US patents and has over 10 pending patents/invention disclosures as an inventor or co-inventor. He has extensive experience in developing products starting from the basic inventions. His research interests include development of meso-, micro- and nanofluidic devices for aerospace, chemical and biotechnology applications.

Dr Raghu is a recipient of the Alexander von Humboldt award from Germany, an Associate Fellow of the AIAA, an invited member of the Special Emphasis Review Panel on Nanotechnology at the National Institutes of Health, US. His passion is in the commercialization of research-generated inventions and has been the Co-Director of Entrepreneurship Workshops in several countries over the last several years.

Richard Brooks

 Richard is a chartered accountant with over 25 years' experience of working with start-ups and SMEs. Richard lives in Cambridge, UK.

Richard qualified at Ernst and Whinney and became Financial Controller of Samuelson Group plc and Finance Director of Samuelson Communications Ltd at the age of 28. In 1990 he moved to Laserpoint Communications Ltd as Finance Director. In 1991 he was appointed as Managing Director as part of an agreement to put the company into administration. He restored its solvency and returned it to its founder a year later when he joined FD Solutions. A co-founder of FD Solutions— a company providing finance director services to companies internationally— Richard's specialist sectors include technology, manufacturing and food. His particular skill-set includes management information systems design and implementation for growing businesses.

Chapter 1

Scientists as entrepreneurs

An entrepreneur is commonly seen as a person who has the skills and initiative to anticipate future needs and who runs a business that brings new products to the market. The entrepreneur accepts the risks involved and benefits from the rewards of a successful venture.

Not many scientists become entrepreneurs. Even scientists with world-beating ideas are rarely motivated to commercialise these for financial gain. It must be self-evident that scientists and entrepreneurs live in very different worlds. Even so, some scientists have broken the mould and become successful entrepreneurs. An inspiring example is Ray Dolby, the US-born physicist who invented the Dolby Noise Reduction system, a technique for reducing hiss originally on tape recordings. In 1965 he started his company, Dolby Laboratories, which developed the Dolby Stereo sound system for cinema. From the 1970s for over 20 years his noise reduction method was used in almost every recording device, which made his company very successful. This book endeavours to answer some of the questions that scientists with an interest in entrepreneurship might ask about taking a novel idea along the path to commercialisation.

Scientist as entrepreneur?

For a scientist considering entrepreneurship, the judgement to make is whether to be the entrepreneur or to join forces with an entrepreneur. But what's the difference between a scientist and an entrepreneur? Is there one?

Creative scientists have curiosity, imagination, good reasoning skills and self-belief. But so do entrepreneurs. So what's the difference? Scientists are often unaware of, or show little interest in, the commercial potential of aspects of their scientific investigations. Entrepreneurs, however, have a keen sense of what an invention might be worth.

This is fine, but it does mean that in past decades scientists have come up with some brilliant, world-beating, millionaire-making inventions and have not been the ones to benefit from them. If you are reading this book you are probably wondering whether it is possible to make some money out of an idea you already have. If this is the case then showing disregard for, or having little interest in, financial matters will not take you very far. It is not possible for anyone to make money out of an idea without some financial acumen.

So what are the necessary attributes of entrepreneurs? Your stereotypical successful entrepreneur is said to be logical, perceptive, organised and responsible, confident, socially extrovert, an excellent communicator, and able to cope with failure.

There are few scientists who have achieved a level of success in their field without being logical, perceptive, organised, responsible and confident. Many scientists have to be excellent communicators or they would never gain the funding they need for their work. Some might even be socially extrovert. All scientists, surely, must be able to cope with failure as no-one's theories or experiments always work out as predicted. However, people who are not entrepreneurs—whether scientists or not—are generally cautious about failure so they would rather not take financial risks.

On the face of it then, the attributes associated with creative scientists and entrepreneurs are not all that different, but there are differences that do appear to be concerned with financial matters. What we are talking about in this book is commercialising inventions. This is what an entrepreneur does—creates products of one sort or another that can be turned into money—and for this you do need 'a head for business'.

Do you have a head for business?

Are you a potential entrepreneur? Consider the following entirely unscientific personality test:

- Do you initiate projects and carry them through?

    Have you had an idea and taken it all the way from idea to product, or do you feel that the interesting part of a project has finished once the idea begins to be commercialised?

- Can you delegate?

    Another way of putting this is 'can you work in a team?' It is important to recognise early on that you are unlikely to have all the skills you need for your project and you will need to, at the very least, pick other people's brains and accept what they tell you. Depending on how far you take your idea, you may need to employ people with skills you neither have nor understand and trust them to do the work you ask them to do.

- Can you be realistic?

    In the course of taking an idea from concept to product you will find everyone doubts you at some time or other, including yourself. Yes, you need to be committed to your idea but you need to be realistic. It's no good giving up just because someone thinks your idea is a bad one if your research says it's okay. But it's also no good flogging a bad idea just because you don't want to prove the doubters right.

- Have you managed projects on your own?
  The buck always stops with the entrepreneur. There is no-one to fall back on. You need to be able to think clearly under pressure, be convincing about your project and your product and be decisive.
- Do you enjoy being in charge?
  Perhaps 'enjoy' is a bit strong, but you do need to be confident and comfortable with responsibility in order to take an idea and make something saleable out of it, no matter what the obstacles might be.
- Could you hire and fire others when necessary?
  It may seem a bit premature to be asking this when all you have at the moment is an idea, but it might in fact be the most important question to answer. If you answer 'no' to this one, this probably means that you are not cut out to run a start-up company. There are other entrepreneurial options that might work better for you.
- Can you criticise other people's work and get them to do what you ask them?
  This is a basic management skill. Again, if you feel that you don't want to work in this type of situation, running a start-up company may not be for you. Be a different type of entrepreneur.
- Are you flexible? Adaptable?
  If you are so wedded to your idea in its current form that you can't change the direction of your research/development when commercial reasons dictate, or you don't feel able to sell your invention for whatever price before the point in its development that you were aiming for, you may not be an entrepreneur.
- Can you negotiate and compromise without feeling that you are selling out?
  'Science' and 'compromise' do not always go together. When developing a product for the market or considering the sale of technology or your company, you may find you have to compromise.
- Can you delay gratification to attain a goal?
  Do you have the determination and patience to wait for the right opportunity to sell your technology or business? Or would you be tempted to sell it at the earliest possible time despite its long-term potential?

An entrepreneur would answer 'yes' to all or certainly most of these questions.

There is no reason why a creative scientist should not be an entrepreneur. It can be personally, professionally and financially very rewarding. If you did not answer 'yes' to most of the questions above or there were areas within those questions that you felt uncomfortable even thinking about, then being an entrepreneur may not be for you. If you're not suited to it, being an entrepreneur can be stressful, demoralising and frustrating. This does not mean that you should give up on any idea or invention that you have. Considering before you start whether you want to be the entrepreneur behind your idea and whether you would be the right person to start a company will help you to decide in which direction you should go with your idea.

Not being the person running the show can be difficult for an inventor to accept, but it is a decision worth getting right. There are other ways of making use of an idea including going into business with someone who is already an entrepreneur. This is an option that will appear again in different forms in this book. There is a saying used in business circles that 'a brilliant idea with poor leadership is less likely to succeed than a moderate idea with good leadership'. If you have a brilliant idea you owe it good leadership.

Is entrepreneurship a gamble?

If you look up the definition of 'entrepreneurship' in almost any dictionary you will find three things mentioned in association with the word: business-venture, risk and profit. If you find the idea of risk exciting read on. If you are terrified by it, please still read on and by the end of the book I hope you will have a better understanding of some of the risks of running a business.

Scientists are used to making decisions based on complete data—for example, a scientist would not apply for a research grant on information that they do not have evidence for. But in contrast an entrepreneur must have the ability to make decisions, such as starting a company, on incomplete data—and that means taking a risk. The decision is made to start a company even though all the factors that could determine its success cannot be known at the time. The information is incomplete. But entrepreneurs do not gamble. They take risks that they have carefully calculated.

Risk must be acceptable. What does this mean? Is the same risk acceptable to one person and not to another? Despite your optimism about the potential success of your business, it is important to consider the position you may find yourself in should it fail. If, for example, you intend to put everything you and your family have into the business and then borrow money that will take the rest of your life on an average salary to repay, imagine what it would be like if the business failed completely and you found yourself with no home or savings and a large debt. That's your worse-case scenario. If this worse-case scenario seems okay to you then taking this degree of risk is 'acceptable' to you. However, if even just thinking about this much loss as a possibility has given you the heebie-jeebies then this is not an acceptable risk for you! In which case you work out what you are prepared to lose should the worst happen. You have to work out for yourself (and you probably need to consult those around you) what is an acceptable risk. Entrepreneurs don't 'gamble' they take 'calculated' and 'acceptable' risks.

Entrepreneurship is about creating a new business. That's all. It's not rocket science. So, any scientist should be able to create one—any scientist who has an idea or invention and a little curiosity about business. The aim of this book is to show you that entrepreneurship can fit well with science.

This book won't tell you how to make a lot of money. It will, though, tell you how to create something saleable out of an invention, and how to make a business out of that. You may make some money out of your business, you may even make a lot of money out of it, but there are no guarantees. You may make a really useful piece of equipment for someone who really needs it, or you might create a few jobs, or you might ultimately change the way something is done. You might fail completely, of course, but that's not the end of the world.

By the end of this book you will have seen different ways to take an invention forward, have enough information to decide if you want to set up a company and have some insight into the risks involved.

What's the big idea?

This book is aimed at creative scientists who already have an idea or an invention and may be considering what to do with it.

Before we go any further let's just be clear that an 'idea' is different from an 'invention'. Going back to rocket scientists for a moment, a new design for a rocket would be an invention. The idea of a rocket is not an invention. An invention should indicate how an idea can be 'reduced to practice'—that is to say that an invention has to indicate by design how the idea can be made to work in practice. An invention may follow on from an idea but you need to have a bit more than just an idea to start a business. You need to have something to sell.

Scientists and engineers, by the nature of what they do, are routinely exposed to new ideas that could be potential inventions. While they clearly recognise the significance of these ideas in their particular area of interest, they often don't consider the application of these ideas in other areas or the possibility of creating saleable products from them. An invention that might be useful in a small way in one field could have a huge market in another area, perhaps one that is, on the face of it, unrelated to 'science'. The result is that a great many ideas that are potential inventions, that could be useful and could have high commercial value, go undeveloped and unexploited for years and sometimes are never developed at all.

The objective of this book is not to show you how to turn an idea into an invention—that's your problem—but to detail the steps that are necessary to turn an invention into something that has commercial value. If you have an idea, consider not just how to turn it into an invention but where the market for it might be. Be creative about ideas that you might have dismissed as they turned out not to have a use in your field. They might have a market appeal somewhere else. If you can reduce the idea to practice then you have an invention and you have the first step towards creating a business.

The next step is to make sure that the invention is, in fact, yours!

Who owns what?

Assuming that you have an idea that you have turned into an invention and you have now decided to do something with it, the first step is to determine who owns it. That might sound ridiculous—it's your idea and you've reduced it to practice. However, take a good look at your terms of employment. They may include a clause that says that anything you invent while working for your employer belongs to your employer.

In a company, generally any inventions made by employees will belong to the company. You might expect this to be the case in research-based companies, but it is in fact the case in many companies. This may even include inventions unrelated to your company's interests that have been made outside company premises. Make sure that you are completely open with your employer and discuss with them what you are doing or intend to do with your invention. In certain circumstances your employer may have no interest in the invention, particularly if it is outside the area of interest of the organisation you work for. If you work for a company developing chemicals for use in agriculture the company may not care if, working in your shed, you have come up with a novel component which improves the sound quality from your phone. In which case they may just tell you to go ahead. Make sure you get this in writing. If your employer is definite that they own the invention they may still not be very interested in the details and you may be able to negotiate with them for ownership, they may agree to own a small percentage of the invention. If your employer owns the invention and wants to keep all of it, this may not be all bad. Responsibility for what happens to the invention from then on will lie with your employer. For instance, your employer becomes responsible for all subsequent expenditure associated with patenting the invention and defending it from patent infringement. This could turn out to be a distinct advantage to you—as you will see in following chapters. You have the benefit of being named as the inventor.

If you work in a university it is likely that the university will own your invention, but it is also likely that everything you need to formalise the existence of your invention will already be easily and practically available to you through the university. Universities nowadays have a lot of experience of protecting and commercialising inventions and you should feel free to make full use of that experience. Most universities now have a technology transfer officer whose job it is to deal with precisely these issues. They will be able to clarify your position as an inventor in relation to your employment contract with the university. It is highly likely that the university will own any invention made by a member of staff and may also own the inventions of research students as well. Many universities encourage spin-out companies and could offer valuable support.

The importance of ownership

The reason why establishing ownership of your invention right from the start is so important is to do with protecting what you have. In the following chapters we will look at how to determine whether an invention can be protected or not and the different methods of protection available. In the meantime it is important to understand why you need to protect your invention.

This book is about the creation of IDEs—Innovation-Driven Enterprises. IDEs are businesses started by entrepreneurs (for instance, you) that are driven by innovation. Innovation is the process of commercialising an invention, i.e. how it can be exploited to give it commercial value. You start with an idea, reduce it to practice and turn it into a product that can be sold. It is in the turning of the invention into a product where the innovation lies. An IDE's most important asset, therefore, is the invention from which its innovation will be derived. It needs to be protected so that no-one else can exploit it. The most common way to protect an invention is to patent it. The patent constitutes the intellectual property of the business. It might be its only asset for quite some time.

It is not just who owns the invention that is important, you also need to determine who the inventor is and if there are any co-inventors. A great many inventions have had input from more than one person. The inventor is the person who contributes significant creative input into the invention. A co-creator is anyone who has made a creative contribution to the invention that is described in at least one claim of a patent application (more later). These are issues that have to be carefully considered before proceeding further.

It might help to consider who is not an inventor:

- Someone who builds your invention according to your specification and design is not an inventor.
- The person you report to (your boss) is not automatically a co-inventor.

These points are important. A patent may be declared invalid if an inventor is excluded from an application. It is also not allowed for someone to be named in the patent application who does not qualify as an inventor. It is not unknown, for example, for a head of department in a university or company to be named as an inventor due to their position, when in fact they have made no novel contribution to the invention. This could invalidate the patent.

The reason why you need to get this right from the start is that patenting an invention (as we will see later) is a time-consuming and lengthy process, the cost of which can be significant. It is also worth realising that only about 3 in 100 granted patents ever end up as successful commercial products[1]. You may already be thinking that you'd rather not bother with patenting, but don't despair. Patenting is essential for scientific entrepreneurship. When a patented product becomes commercially successful the rewards can be significant.

Here is an example, which is perhaps an extreme one when we're talking about start-ups, but one worth quoting. A few years ago Kodak, the company that invented the digital camera, went bankrupt. Yet their patent portfolio of over 1000 patents was sold to various companies for over $500 million. So how do you arrive at a valuation like this?

WIPO (the World Intellectual Property Organisation) mention four factors that help determine the value of a patent.

1. The importance of the patent

   Breakthrough patents which can be applied to a number of new areas of technology, such as Edison's light bulb or the photocopier, have very high value. Such patents protect the owner from competition for a long time over large sectors of industry and can be worth billions. On the other hand, patents which make only an incremental difference to existent technology are the least valuable, for example, adding a voice to a plastic toy doll. So, how a

---

[1] (Stuart West, intellectual property lawyer based in Walnut Creek, California quoted in Marton Dunai, 'More inventors try to market products,' *Oakland Tribune*, September 5, 2006)

competitor views the nature of a patent will determine what they are prepared to pay for it.

2. The market

   Another significant factor in determining the value of a patent is the size of the business opportunity that the invention presents, i.e. what are the sales that can be achieved and for how long while the patent is in force.

3. The patent term

   Patents have a maximum term of 20 years and, therefore, afford the owner a monopoly potentially of 20 years. However, certain products can take a long time to progress from invention to launch. Medical products not uncommonly can take 8–10 years so that the monopoly period left is now about 10 years. Further, a patent nearing the end of its term is likely to itself meet competition from other novel technologies which will reduce its value.

4. Prior art

   When applying for a patent you are required to describe the 'prior art', that is you need to reference other patents that are similar to yours and then indicate why your invention is novel. The number of patents in your area of innovation will affect the value of your patent. It is evident that if a product based on your invention is one of many such products the customer will have a wide choice of products which consequently reduces the value of every patent in that area. On the other hand, a stand-alone patent, i.e. one with few or no competitors and, therefore, a monopoly over a large customer base, will command a much higher premium.

   The costly and lengthy nature of patenting is why you might be pleased to find that the university you work for will own the invention and therefore be responsible for the patent. Let's say that an invention patented by a university is successfully commercialised and the income from it is received by the university in the form of royalties. This royalty income is usually distributed between the university and the inventor, with the larger percentage going to the university. This might seem a bit unfair when 'the university' has not contributed anything to the invention itself, until you realise that the university as the owner of the patent has to pay the annual patent renewal fees out of their share of the royalties. These renewal fees may need to be paid for 20 years. Even worse, the university as owner of the patent has to deal with any infringement of the patent and bear the legal costs. This could be extremely expensive. It is not surprising that the university usually takes a larger percentage of any royalty income received.

   The next question should be: does the invention have potential?

Will it work?

How would you know? You may think it's the best invention in the world but there may be such significant obstacles in the way of bringing it to market that it's not worth pursuing. What can help is to conduct a risk/benefit analysis.

Take, for example, the potential development of a non-invasive blood glucose device. At the present time diabetics prick their fingers to obtain blood samples to find out their blood glucose concentrations. This can be painful and means the measurements may not be taken as often as would be beneficial. An alternative approach is to develop a non-invasive device which measures the blood glucose concentration without the need for drawing a blood sample. A risk/benefit analysis might look something like this:

Benefit	Risk
Huge business opportunity: 200 million diagnosed diabetics worldwide.	Technically extremely difficult to produce a reliable instrument.
Funding is available via grants, and investors show interest.	The need to regularly calibrate the device. Long time to product launch.
No current competition.	Potentially significantly higher device cost than the currently used devices.
Acceptance of the proposed instrument by potential customers is highly likely.	

Another way of expressing the risk/benefit factors of your invention is to present its strengths and weaknesses in a SWOT (strengths, weaknesses, opportunities and threats) analysis. A SWOT analysis is a method used to evaluate the chances of success of a product or enterprise. Strengths and weaknesses are internal factors and opportunities and threats are external. A SWOT analysis of the non-invasive glucose instrument project might look like this:

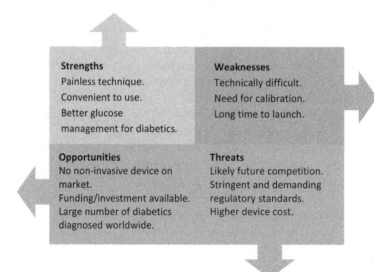

- Strengths: these are factors that will give the invention an advantage over others.
  Examples of strengths are patents, brand names, cost advantage, access to distributors.
- Weaknesses: these are factors that put the invention at a disadvantage compared to others.
  Examples of weaknesses are no patent protection, high costs, lack of distribution networks.
- Opportunities: possibilities for the invention that can be exploited to its advantage.
  Examples of opportunities are an identified customer need, new technology, need stimulated by legislation.
- Threats: external factors that can significantly reduce the chances of success of the invention.
  Examples of threats are competitive products, new regulatory requirements that affect the products.

The way to use a SWOT diagram is as a thought experiment to systematically list all the positives and negatives in the enterprise. This should help you to make the decision whether to go ahead with an enterprise such as a start-up company.

Do you want to start a company?

There—we've said it: 'start a company'. We'll accept that you would like to take your idea and turn it into something tangible, but do you want to run a company? We can go into the practicalities of starting a company later in the book, but for the moment consider whether you see yourself running a company that may employ a number of people. If the answer is 'yes' you do want to start a company, an important question to ask yourself is 'why'? You might think these are the same reasons as being an entrepreneur, but they are not. You can be an entrepreneur without starting a company. There are many reasons for starting a company but make sure that you've examined yours carefully to avoid being misled into having unrealistic expectations. Let's consider the reasons people give:
- Being your own boss. Yes, certainly, starting a company may enable you to run the operation your way. But the flip-side of that is you'll be responsible for your decisions and if the business fails it will be your responsibility to deal with the consequences. In your own company you'll have to work with others as a team, a skill not everyone possesses.
- Financial gain. There is no guarantee that a company will make money, let alone a lot of money. But it is possible. The idea of starting a company to be better off financially is clearly attractive but remember that this is in no way guaranteed. Also, the success of a company can mean different things to different people—the profit it generates, the number of jobs it creates, or the benefit it brings to the scientific community or to your local community. Many small innovation-driven companies make an impact worldwide.

Whether you ultimately decide to start a company is probably determined by 'acceptable' risk, as has been described. You may never want to get involved in a high risk/high reward start-up IDE. It may be that you are a creative scientist with an entrepreneurial inclination but with no desire, for whatever reason, to start your own company and be responsible for employing other people. What, then, are your options?

In the course of this book we will examine the different ways in which an invention can be exploited, from licensing a patent to deciding to start a company and many options in between. We will look at how an IDE can raise money and how to estimate how much money needs to be raised. We will explain how to assess the business opportunity that an invention presents and how to write a business plan to make the most of that opportunity. We will not, by the way, tell you how to run a company on a day-to-day basis, there are many other books that can help you do that.

What we 'will' ask you is, having taken the decision to start on the exploitation of your invention, how will you finish it? In other words, what is your 'exit route'? We will be taking a closer look at this question in the next chapter.

Chapter 2

Selling your invention—options 1 and 2

You have so far established that you are a creative scientist with entrepreneurial flair and you have an invention, or an idea that could become an invention. You may not, though, want to get involved in a high risk/high reward start-up company—an Innovation-Driven Enterprise—at this stage in your scientific career.

Let's take a look at what you might be able to do with no more than an invention and some experimental data, that is to say, what is the commercial path you can take to get a reward for your assets, whatever these may be—inventions, time, or hard graft. In business terms, an exit route is the method by which you and your investors would realise their investment. It is the means by which you end your involvement with your invention, or with a company that you may have developed from it. However, you don't even need to have a company to take an exit route. You can have a go at selling your invention before you get anywhere near the stage of creating an actual company. If you go down this route, your return is likely to be much smaller than the return that you could get at a later date when you have, say, a start-up company or perhaps even with a product.

Your commercial options

What, then, are your commercial options as an inventor? There are four:
1. Sell your unpatented invention at the earliest opportunity.
2. Patent your invention, demonstrate proof-of-principle, then sell it.
3. Put your invention in a start-up company, develop a prototype device, then sell the company.
4. Go on to manufacture your product in your start-up.

In this chapter we will consider the pros and cons of the first two options. We'll look at options 3 and 4 in the next chapter.

Option 1: Sell your unpatented invention

One possible early exit route is to find a company whose core business might benefit from your invention and who might take it off your hands before you have patented it. You would be looking for a company who would have the finances, facilities and ability to take your invention, patent it, develop it into one or more products and then commercialise them. This is not an easy exit route to pull off but if you don't want to patent your invention yourself but can see that it has the perfect place in a particular company then it may be worth having a go.

Remember, to gain the interest of a company, any new product that the company went on to develop from your invention would have to offer advantages over other, related products already commercially available, or your invention would have to offer the interested company a new, significant, business opportunity altogether. You will need to do your research thoroughly into the company's market and what your invention could contribute to it before making any approach. It may be blindingly obvious to you what your invention can do for them but it might not be so clear to a busy company executive who has agreed to give you 10 minutes of their time.

Bear in mind that few companies may be willing to undertake the necessary research and development to create a saleable product from an unpatented invention. To most companies, an invention without a patent has not been tested for originality. So the chances of success with this approach are not high but are worth looking into because there are always exceptions. There are cases where a company will be prepared to take on the development and the costs of filing the patent application if they can see a good enough product or market opportunity at the end of it. A strictly marketing company, for example, even one selling products from your area of technology, is unlikely to respond positively to an approach from you. They won't have the necessary development and manufacturing facilities.

Do your research, keep an eye on the business press to see which companies may be moving into your area of interest, and remember that it would be to your benefit to find more than one company with an interest in your invention. This would at least create some competition which would be to your advantage.

A few years ago I (DP) invented a device for measuring the oxygen partial pressure in an extracorporeal loop for use during open heart surgery. I did not immediately patent it. At a medical trade show I approached one of the owners of a company whose core business was in this area. After a long discussion at the show we entered into a confidentiality agreement and spent a few weeks discussing the invention and how we might work together on developing it. We agreed on a technology transfer in which I assigned my invention to the company. For this I was paid an upfront fee and also entered into a consultancy agreement with them. They took on the responsibility for applying for a patent and doing the development work right up to the launch of the product. My consultancy agreement with them lasted throughout this period and for 2 years after the product was launched. This is not a common experience, but it can happen.

Making contact

Gaining access to the people in any company you wish to contact about your invention is often difficult. However, as I have just demonstrated, trade shows and scientific conferences can be very useful places to make contacts. Anyone with an interest in medical devices, for example, might benefit from a trip to Medtec Europe (http://www.medteceurope.com/). Trade shows for other industries are listed at: http://www.eventseye.com. When attending a trade show decide which of the exhibiting companies might be interested in your invention and plan your visit around them. These trade shows are huge and you can waste a lot of time and energy if you are not prepared. Try to find out in advance who you could speak to from a particular company and arrange an appointment with them at the show. *Do not feel tempted to divulge any proprietary information to them about your invention.* Keep any discussions to what your invention can do rather than how it does it, or you might lose the right to patent it in the future. If at all possible try to gain access to the most senior member of staff present on a company's trade stand, preferably management, or at least get their email addresses. If you are not able to do this, or you happen to be at the show and spot an interesting company you hadn't thought about in advance, at the very least talk to the sales people on the trade stand about what you are doing and ask for the email addresses of the most useful contacts for you.

Note: However comfortable you may feel talking to them, it is probably not a good idea to make your approach to a company through the scientists or engineers—unless, of course, you know them personally and they are willing to help you out. Scientists and engineers who have never heard of you may not have much patience with your invention, particularly as you are not going to be able to divulge the most interesting parts of it to them without the protection of a patent. Worse, they may feel that your invention is something they should have thought up themselves! So, expect a negative response.

Large scientific conferences will often have an area devoted to a trade show specific to the subject of the conference. Whenever you attend a scientific conference make a point of visiting the trade stands and talking to the people there. You may find a company exhibiting that you have not come across before that has its core business in the area of your research or invention—or they may know a company that might be interested. Try to find out the contact details for the person in the company who is responsible for bringing in new technology. Any approach to a company is more likely to succeed if it is made to the R&D Director or the CEO. Finding out who they are is usually as simple as googling 'R&D Director of...'. For a UK company you can contact Companies House to find out who the company directors are. Most countries have a similar organisation through which you can identify who might be useful to contact in any particular company.

Be shameless about using colleagues, friends and family to get contact names or introductions into companies that might be helpful to you. A personal introduction or recommendation is worth any amount of unsolicited emails.

When making any approach it is important to be able to make a quick and early impact on the person you are explaining your invention to, especially if they are company executives. Imagine that you had to explain your invention to them during a short trip in a lift (elevator), say 30 seconds or a little more ('elevator pitch'). Write the email approach you make in this way as well. An elaborate and detailed description of your idea or invention is unlikely to have a successful impact and, of course should be avoided as you don't have a patent in place. Remember, the person who makes the ultimate decision about bringing new inventions into a company is unlikely to be a scientist, and even if they are they may not be a specialist in your field. They are much more likely to have a background in sales than at the coal-face of innovation. Tell them how your invention can benefit their company. Senior executives do not generally reply to individual inventors who have emailed them unless what you tell them could make a significant difference to their business, and in order for them to take notice of you, you will need to tell them what you have to say in very, very few words.

Non-disclosure

Assuming that you get one or more positive responses from companies, you will need to protect your invention as much as you can before revealing anything specific. Get each interested company to sign your (or their) Non-Disclosure Agreement (NDA) before you reveal the details of your invention to them. While you will find many examples of NDAs on the internet, it is best to have such an agreement written for you and for your particular circumstances by a qualified person such as a lawyer. You can, of course, sign an NDA offered by the recipient (e.g. the interested company) you are dealing with if their terms are acceptable to you but it is still advisable to check their terms with a lawyer. Realise, too, that you are also bound by the NDA not to disclose any confidential information that you may have received from the recipient. It is quite common to make the duration of the NDA 3–5 years.

If they do show an interest, what you then get out of it is subject to commercial negotiation, i.e. you need to work this out with the company. The company is most likely to provide you with a standard company agreement which you can then work on with them (and with a solicitor with commercial experience). Assuming that your invention is a significant one, a typical deal is for an upfront fee to be paid for the invention plus royalties and possibly the offer of a consultancy.

Any company taking on an unpatented invention will be incurring significant costs in patenting it, protecting the patent, and developing the invention into a product. They know that they will be putting much more into the development of your invention than you put into it in the first place, so don't expect a huge payment for your invention.

The upfront fee

The fee paid at the signing of an agreement for your invention is negotiable and depends on many factors such as the business opportunity your invention presents to the company, the likelihood of the successful development of a product, the time to the launch of the product and the likelihood of getting a patent granted on the invention.

It is quite difficult to put a value on an invention for which a patent application has not been filed. Everything then depends on what you are able to negotiate with a company. Without a patent it is unlikely that an invention is going to earn you a life-changing sum of money. Think of it more as a bonus, a figure that perhaps represents a percentage of your salary.

Once a fee is agreed and paid, the company will become owners of the invention and the decision to protect the invention by filing a patent application is then their responsibility. You will be 'the named inventor' in a patent application, but you will have no ownership of the invention after the deal (the US is an exception). The company may agree to you submitting the invention and experimental results for publication, but only at a later date, after they have filed a patent application. Before signing such an agreement get good tax advice. This could be to your financial benefit.

Consultancy

After the purchase of your invention the company is likely to invite you to be a consultant since they would almost certainly want the assurance of your continuing involvement during the years of research and development that will be necessary for them to develop your invention into a product. This is true for all three commercial options (above). Apart from the income that could result from such a consultancy it is worth noting that an involvement like this with a commercial company has other benefits. As a consultant, you are also likely to have access to proprietary scientific information which would not normally be published. Consultancies, particularly with major international companies, can improve your academic reputation and career prospects.

When the collaborating company presents you with their proposed consultancy contract for your consideration and signature it is advisable to discuss this firstly with your employer. In a university you will need to consult the university's legal department to see how a consultancy with a commercial company would impact on your terms of employment. An agreement may be reached between you and the university in which you are able to work flexibly to fit your consultancy hours around your research and teaching commitments. In many cases consultancy tasks are carried out outside 'office hours' in which case the university may wish not to be involved. Once these issues are cleared up it would also be advisable to consult your solicitor about the terms of the consultancy agreement and the remuneration on offer.

Your consultancy will depend on various factors such as your availability and your ability to communicate effectively with a multi-disciplinary company team. The ability to communicate well is an essential skill required by most companies and you are likely to be judged by it. Can you successfully and succinctly explain your invention to a group of scientists? Yes? Now can you do it to the company accountants? You may find you need to explain the value of your invention to company marketing people who will not be at all interested in the fascinating technical aspects of why your invention has been taken up by their company. You will undoubtedly need to be able to collaborate with a team of people, which means sharing everything you know about your invention. Some scientists and inventors find this difficult. Also remember that, as part of a consultancy agreement, any reports you submit to the company will be subject to the consultancy agreement. This means that the information in them will be confidential (even though you might feel as though it belongs to you as the inventor) and will be the property of the recipient company. You will not be able to discuss these confidential matters with your colleagues or friends.

Consultancy fees are normally paid at a rate per day with a minimum number of days per month stated in such an agreement. Again, the fees you are able to get from the collaborating company and the duration of the agreement will depend on many factors but this is a personal matter and depends very much on what you will be happy with and what is likely to stimulate you to do your best for the project. It is worth noting that asking for a low daily rate because you want to be helpful, or you already have a full-time job and are treating this as a bit of a hobby, is not necessarily a good idea. It is not unknown for your reputation in your field to be judged by the fees you command. To give you an example, a few years ago I (DP) was a consultant to a major multi-national company earning what I thought was quite a nice daily rate. One of their directors helpfully told me that my reports made no impact on the Board of Directors of the company. He explained that the highly paid board of directors was not accustomed to taking advice from someone they paid such a derisory daily rate to. As a result of this discussion my daily rate was made more appropriate(!) and my reports were taken much more seriously!

A further issue that might come up is the one of exclusivity, that is to say the requirement that you should act as a consultant to this particular company and no other. As a research scientist you clearly have specialist expertise in your particular field, but as a creative scientist it is also likely that you have inventive ideas in areas well outside your area of research. In such a situation you would clearly want the opportunity to consult for other companies in these other areas. It would be advisable to indicate to any company that approaches you regarding consultancy that while you are happy to act as a consultant to that company in the area of the particular invention they are interested in, you would want a non-exclusive agreement which would enable you to be free to consult with other companies in different, non-conflicting areas.

One final point about consultancies. In my (DP) experience it has been the consultancy work I have done for companies that has been of most help later when looking for companies to collaborate with or to sell other inventions to. I had already done consultancy work for several major pharmaceutical companies before I started my first company. The contacts you make when working as a consultant can be invaluable. On the other hand, you may be wondering how much easier it might be to interest companies in your invention if you patent it first.

Option 2: Patent and demonstrate proof-of-principle

Let's now consider the second commercial option. In this option you would apply for a patent on your invention, demonstrate proof-of-principle and then sell it. It is certainly the case that you are more likely to succeed in interesting a company in your invention if you've already filed a patent application and have experimental results which prove the principle of your invention. If you can show proof-of-principle with a laboratory (garage?) set-up then that's fine, even if it is a 'rat's nest' of wires in a cardboard box. Whatever it looks like at this early stage, it is important that your laboratory set-up is good enough to demonstrate that the invention works.

There are many companies, particularly the larger ones, that are happy to leave fundamental research and development to smaller companies or individual research-ers and inventors. This gives these large companies the possibility of acquiring novel technologies from external sources rather than setting up extensive R&D facilities in-house. They are generally more interested in novel technology not only for which proof-of-principle has been demonstrated, but for which a patent has been filed, or granted. Both of these are positive steps on the path to commercialisation of the invention.

We will be looking at the patent process itself in detail in a later chapter. A patent application and any other Intellectual Property (IP), such as know-how, associated with your invention have value. Your job is to find the person or company that wants to buy it.

Public disclosure

Before we go any further let's look at confidentiality. In the time before you file your patent application, e.g. while you are obtaining proof-of-principle and while you are working with your patent lawyer in drafting the patent application, it is in your interests not to disclose any details about your invention.

If you need to discuss your invention with anyone, make sure that they sign an NDA. If you disclose any details about your invention to anyone without such an agreement the information you have divulged would be considered as being in the 'public domain' and you will then not be able to patent the invention.

Any such disclosure, for instance telling a friend, discussing your invention with a colleague, presenting it at a scientific meeting or seminar, sending an abstract to a conference, publishing a paper, a press release, an advertisement, releasing infor-mation on a website or blog, or sending a sample of your invention to anyone, will constitute public disclosure so that you will then not be able to patent the invention. In such a situation you can, of course, publish the details about your invention and get the academic benefit from the publication, but a patent will not be possible.

Selling your intellectual property

The companies most likely to show an interest in your invention are those whose core business is directly in the area of the technology of your invention. Also, you need to be talking to companies with the in-house facilities to take the development of your invention to product stage. Keep an eye on the business press to see which companies are moving into your area of interest. It would be to your benefit to interest more than one company in your invention as competition among them will be to your advantage.

Let's assume, then, that you've found a company that is interested in your invention, what do you do next? Even though you've applied for a patent on your invention, it is still advisable to require anyone interested in your invention to sign an NDA.

Non-disclosure agreements

The same general information about NDAs applies for option 2 as for option 1. There are occasions when, having signed the NDA and having reviewed your invention, the recipient will argue that they are not bound by the restrictions in the NDA since the invention was already known to them at the time of the disclosure. They may even have been working on the concept themselves. This might be the case, but it would be entirely reasonable for you to request evidence from them of this such as a signed and dated laboratory notebook showing their record of the invention.

A particularly sticky issue to resolve is what would happen if there is a significant dispute about any of the terms in the NDA. It is often the case that in a dispute between the parties to the agreement, the Recipient is likely to require that the dispute be settled in their country according to the laws of their country. This could be a very expensive concession to make. Settling such a case in a court in another country could be a formidable and expensive exercise. Unfortunately, if you are dealing with a major company you may have no alternative. This situation apart, it is important to have an NDA which is written with maximum clarity to minimise the possibility of disagreements.

Once you have both agreed upon and signed your NDA, then you can enter into in-depth discussions with the company about your invention. You can now reveal the details of your invention. This will involve telling them what the exact problem is that your invention addresses, what is novel about your solution, and how you believe it fits into their company strategy. You would also know that your invention addresses a significant market.

At this point the company may well ask you to give them a prototype of your invention for them to try out. This would have to be something well-constructed and robust, a demonstrator that can be handled successfully by other people. A prototype needs to be something fairly neat-looking that would stand being sent by post or courier, possibly to a different country. It does not need to look like a finished product and it would not be unreasonable to ask the company to pay you for it.

If the company confirms that the prototype demonstrates your invention, that your invention addresses a problem, and that the cost of components for a final product would be within their requirements, then you may well be at the point where the company would offer you a deal for your invention. This might be in the form of a licence, or they might want to buy your invention and all of the IP associated with it. A further part of the deal you strike with the company will almost certainly be their requirement for you to continue to be involved as a consultant with the development of the product(s) resulting from the invention. The duration of such a consultancy is likely to be until the company engineers are able to completely continue the product development in-house.

Licensing agreement

In a licensing agreement the licensee pays you, the inventor, upfront for the assignment of the rights to commercialise your invention. This payment is made at the time of the agreement long before development or sales of the product have started. This can be a fee for the licence paid upfront plus royalties which are payments made to the licensor that are based on sales of the product. More commonly, the up-front payment is an advance made against future royalties. So it's easy to see that for the inventor, royalties are an important part of a licensing agreement, so that both the licensee and the inventor could achieve significant income.

It is reasonable to negotiate for the payment of a royalty on the sale of all products which are based on your invention. The lifetime of a patent in most countries is 20 years so if it takes, say, 5 years to launch the product from the signing of the licence agreement then you would expect to receive royalties for 15 years. This assumes, of course, that the products are still selling by then!

Generally speaking, royalties of 1%–4% of the end-user price is what companies pay for products that sell in high volume. The end-user price is the price that the ultimate purchaser pays. For consumer products the end-user will be the public. In other situations it might be an organisation which is buying your product, in which case the end-user price would be the listed price before any negotiated discount. For high end-user value products which may sell in smaller volume, the royalties can be up to 6%–8%. Make sure that the end-user price you will be receiving commission on is the price *listed* by the company, not the price *charged* by the company. In some cases, companies might use your product as a free giveaway in order to promote another product, so you could be earning a percentage royalty on zero sales income!

Licence agreements can be either exclusive or non-exclusive. In the former case, commercialisation rights are assigned to only one company; in the latter, rights can be assigned to a number of companies usually for use of the invention in different areas of application or in different countries. For example, an invention may have an application in the automotive industry but its use could also be beneficial in food manufacture. In such a situation a non-exclusive licence could be granted to two companies each applying the technology in their own area of interest. In such a non-exclusive licensing agreement the upfront fee paid by each licensee will be lower than for an exclusive licence. However, you could have many such non-exclusive upfront licence payments if your invention has the possibility of various applications.

There is one other important issue that the licence agreement should address. You need to ensure that you assign licensing rights to a company that has the definite intention to sell a product or products based on your invention. Their putting your invention 'on the shelf' will obviously not benefit you. It is advisable, therefore, to insert clauses in the agreement which require annual minimum sales to be achieved. If these annual sales are not achieved the rights to the invention should revert to you, if you can negotiate that!

We then come to the sticky question of the size of the upfront fee. Here there are no rules or guidelines for determining such numbers. What may be possible is to ask for a sum equal to the projected first year's sales of the products based on your invention. Try that! But remember that it needs to be a figure that is acceptable not only to you but is also reasonable for the company to accept. If, for example, their cost of marketing and selling your novel product are so high in the first year that they make a loss on the first year sales, would you still insist on an upfront licence fee equal to first year sales? Put yourself in their shoes and test if what you are asking for is also reasonable from their point of view. What might be a good compromise is to ask for an annual payment based on agreed annual minimum sales, whether achieved or not.

An IP sale

When the company decides to buy your IP rather than opt for a licence agreement they will most likely provide you with their standard IP sale agreement. This is just a starting point. You do not have to go along with what this agreement says. It is up to you to negotiate the final terms.

In any negotiations, you have to proceed on the basis that there is goodwill on both sides. Any issues you have with what the company is offering or with the conditions they are imposing can only be resolved if both you and the company are willing to work on resolving them.

Rather than an upfront fee, some inventors opt to receive research and development funding instead so that they can undertake the further development of their invention themselves. For instance, they might ask for financial support to fund research in their laboratory. This approach would probably be preferable for those scientists interested in an academic career in research and development rather than in financial gain. Bear in mind that there could also be a consultancy contract for the inventor.

In many cases it would be better to get an independent advisor to do these negotiations for you. The problem is that a researcher very often thinks in terms of the money that was spent making the invention and proving the principle. This might have been a relatively small outlay, and it is not uncommon for the inventor to negotiate a fee for their invention based on a small multiple of this outlay. Quite the opposite, an upfront fee should be based on the value of the invention, i.e. the business opportunity that such an invention offers the company you are negotiating with. This is an area where it would be useful to gain the advice of someone who has experience of putting a value on the business opportunity that an invention offers. An accountant should be able to recommend someone to you who has experience in your field to help you to work out a realistic value.

An example of a situation where an independent advisor might have been useful is an incident that happened to me (DP) a few years ago. A fellow physicist and family friend was staying for the weekend. I knew that a company I had had previous dealings with were trying to solve a particular problem. My friend and I worked out a solution to this problem over breakfast and felt very pleased with ourselves for having come up with a solution within half an hour. We phoned the company with our solution and they immediately offered us what we, at the time, considered a significant reward if we could demonstrate the operation of our solution at their premises. We put together a very simple demonstrator and took it to the company's premises a few days later. The demonstration was successful and we felt triumphant. The company gave us our reward and we were very pleased with ourselves. The company now has the device incorporated into a larger system and its incorporation has made their system unique in the marketplace. In retrospect, the reward we got was handsome in terms of the time we had spent on it but nothing like its market value. What a mistake!

If you do decide to do your own negotiations, be clear about what you want to achieve but also bear in mind that the other party—the company buying your IP—also has requirements. For instance, the company may only sell products online which means that your invention must ultimately be easily transportable without risk of damage. If, for instance, your invention is to be carried around all day in a handbag, it's no good offering a solution that weighs a few kilos and has no potential for weight reduction. In such a situation the buying company will have to commit to further development and investment after buying your IP. They may see this as a disincentive and decline the opportunity. Keeping all of this in mind means that you can better understand what leverage you might have in the negotiations and what you may have to concede. You could help the negotiations along in this particular case by indicating to the company that you have ideas for reducing the cost and possibly the size of the production units that they are intending to produce in volume. Your ideas may well be accepted and result in an offer from the company for you to act as their consultant in this area.

If, in your discussions with the company, it looks like an agreement might be possible, do not make any commitments until you've sought the advice of a solicitor or lawyer. The advice of an accountant would also be helpful not just for tax implications but also for determining the financial credibility of the company you are dealing with.

Ultimately, what you require is a well-drafted IP sale agreement to avoid disagreements later. What you want to avoid is ending up in a legal dispute to resolve ambiguities and omissions. A court will pay attention to the words in an agreement and not to the intention of the parties who signed it.

What to be aware of in an IP sale agreement

There are some items that are common to most IP sale agreements which it would be as well to be aware of:

Confidential information

With the sale of your intellectual property (which consists of your invention, patent application, know-how and experimental results) comes the requirement that you will keep the details of your IP confidential, along with the details of the deal itself. Although it is likely that the company will agree to your publishing details of your invention (since you've already filed a patent application) the agreement is likely to require you to obtain the permission of the company for any further publications or presentations at conferences. If the invention is a major part of your research area, this can be a difficult issue to resolve. It may be that you will get permission to publish or disclose the results of further research with certain 'proprietary information' (of commercial value but not considered necessary to publish in a science journal) omitted. This may not be to your satisfaction but could be a consequence of such a commercial transaction and you may just have to accept this.

An example could be that you have sold your invention of a sensor for detecting a particular gas. The company you have sold this to may agree to your publishing a paper on your invention but only if you agree to exclude the 'proprietary information' such as the exact insulating material you used or the temperature cycle you subjected the sensor to which you discovered during your research. Without this information anyone reading your paper will not be able to successfully reproduce your device nor will you be in a position at a conference, or anywhere else for that matter, to explain their inability to reproduce your work. Your credibility could suffer.

Some years ago, I (DP) invented an electrochemical oxygen sensor incorporated in the tip of a catheter just over 1 mm in diameter. The anode and cathode of the device were separated by less than 0.3 mm of epoxy resin. A number of scientific papers were published describing this device, which was being commercially produced and was performing very successfully *in vivo* in premature babies. However, people who attempted to make such a device for themselves from the details in the published papers found that there was high leakage current between the electrodes and the device was extremely unstable. The conclusion they made was that the device I had invented was not functional. I can recall more than one conference where these remarks were made in my presence. I was unable to participate in these discussions because of the confidentiality restrictions on me—I could not reveal certain proprietary information. The proprietary information that I was not allowed to publish was quite simple; the device needed to be exposed to gamma radiation to increase the resistance of the epoxy resin between the cathode and anode to keep the leakage current negligibly small. When used in premature babies obviously the device was sterilised, by gamma radiation. Anyone who made the device for an objective that did not require sterilisation would quite rightly have found that it did not work reliably!

Confidentiality applies not only to you and your invention and the subsequent results you generate for the company, but also applies in the opposite direction. The information you learn from the company about your invention, its technical input to the development of the product, the results of its market surveys, market analysis and the business opportunity that the product offers, together with the company's strategy for the sale of the product, all constitute confidential information which will fall under this agreement. You will not be free to disclose any of this information.

Non-competition clauses

Non-competition clauses are likely to be included in an IP sale agreement which restrict the inventor from competing with the recipient company. What this means is that this will prevent you from collaborating with others—companies or individuals—on exploiting other technologies that will compete with the products resulting from your IP. The non-competition clause may also require that any further development or modification of your invention which you may be researching, or indeed any subsequent invention you come up with that could make the original invention obsolete, must be reported to the company and the ownership of this information assigned to the company. For many research scientists this may be a deal breaker because it will clearly put any further research publications under significant restrictions or may, at worst, cause a problem in continuing in that particular area of research. If you, as the inventor, are prepared to agree to terms that could cause you difficulties in the future with your work or your prospects, then it would seem reasonable for you to be compensated not only for the IP they are buying but for any future related IP and for any detriment you may suffer by these non-competition clauses.

The end product

In an IP sale, consider that your invention may have many applications, not just the one that you've thought of. It would be in your interests to negotiate an IP sale agreement in which the acquiring company has the exclusive right to use the invention in their area of application in order to create the product they want from it, but that you retain the right to use the principle of the invention in all other possible applications. For example, the acquiring company may have the right to use your invention in agriculture, but you retain the right to use it for everything else. This may not be easy to agree but it may be a compromise position if there is an intractable disagreement about payment for your invention.

I (DP) have always had an interest in selling IP, but my preferred route has tended to be through an intellectual property company (IPC). This is option 3, and we will discuss this, along with option 4, in the next chapter.

IOP Publishing

Entrepreneurship for Creative Scientists

Dawood Parker, Surya Raghu and Richard Brooks

Chapter 3

Selling your invention—options 3 and 4

I (DP) have had some success at running what might be called a sort of halfway house to running a 'real' company, what I would call an intellectual property company (IPC) or a company of inventions. In the sense that we will be using it here, an IPC is a company which comes up with an idea, turns it into an invention, protects the IP—usually by filing a patent application—undertakes the research, develops the invention to proof-of-principle stage and finally develops an engineering prototype which can be demonstrated. This is the third option open to creative scientists who have an idea and wish to exploit it.

Option 3: Create a start-up company, develop a prototype and sell the company

An IPC is most suited to those scientists who consider themselves good at inventing but don't feel that they have a head for business, or would rather focus on research and inventing than launching a full-scale business.

I (DP) have been associated with three IPCs which were subsequently acquired by major companies. In all of these, patent applications had been filed and proof-of-principle was confirmed. The financial rewards of this approach can be significant. As with any start-up company you have to fund the running of the company until it is sold. At least with this approach the reward, if it happens, occurs much earlier than with a conventional start-up company committed to production, marketing and sales. The IPC approach, the halfway house, is not at all an unattractive option.

It is based on the further realisation that creative scientists, given the favourable environment in which they work, can have ideas which are outside their specific research areas and often outside the terms of their employment. For example, if you are employed in the area of nanotechnology, your invention of mowing your lawn using laser beams(!) is your own for which your employer (for example a University) would be unlikely to lay claim to.

doi:10.1088/978-0-7503-1146-5ch3

Why start an IPC?

The straightforward answer is grant funding. Grants are available in many countries to support or encourage innovation. The UK government, for example, has several options available for people in various stages of product development: www.gov.uk/innovation-get-support-and-advice. To qualify for this type of grant support in the UK, and probably elsewhere, you will need to be a 'legal entity' i.e. you have to have started a company. In general, these grants are for larger amounts of funding than research grants. There are other incentives for start-up companies such as financial assistance in setting up premises, equipment grants, contributions towards employee salaries, travel grants, help with patent costs and so on. These grants are not available to inventors as private individuals. This can make all the difference in enabling you to take an invention from proof-of-principle to prototype stage and to attract interest in your invention from companies.

It is also the case that many larger companies are not involved in research and are quite prepared to acquire IP for new products from IPCs. For instance, a company you are undertaking some consultancy work for may let you know that they are seeking the solution to a problem and would be quite happy to buy that solution from your IPC should you solve it for them. Finding out what companies need is not always easy and the contacts you make through consultancy work can be invaluable. Alternatively, websites such as 'Innocentive Challenge' can give you some idea of the problems companies are interested in solving. Government funding organisations can also give you a good idea of where further research or innovation is required, particularly when they announce calls for funding in specific areas. For this to be a viable approach for you it is necessary to determine that your invention addresses a significant market—it must offer the acquiring company a large business opportunity. For example, do you have ideas for developing a battery that will extend the range of an electric car to many hundreds of kilometres? Can you think of a way of detecting the presence of any explosive material from a long distance away? A solution to problems like these, even if they are developed in your garage, will find you a buyer in no time and the price will be high, very high. If you were fortunate to have solutions to such problems in your IPC, you would have many major companies beating a path to your door.

In an IPC, what you will not need to concern yourself with are regulatory matters associated with your product, manufacturing, sales and, of course, the management of a team of employees. You may at some stage need the help of another scientist or engineer with workshop facilities to build your prototype. But soon after that you will be in a position with your prototype to demonstrate that your invention works. The possibility that a company will then be interested in acquiring your IPC could be quite high. That, after all, was your objective in taking the IPC route.

Selling your IPC

When selling your company, the obvious question that arises is 'what is it worth?'. The answer I've (DP) received many times, having been in this position a few times is 'how long is a piece of string?'. In my view, this is a very unhelpful and confused response since a tape measure would solve that question quite easily. Determining the value of an IPC with any accuracy is not possible. Let's imagine this IPC has one invention in it. Unlike the piece of string, where only length is involved, the value of an IPC depends on many factors such as the extent of its IP—not just the patent but the know-how—the cost of further research and development of the product and the time these will require before launch of the product, the marketing and sales costs (always high for a novel product) to name but a few.

What you don't do is think of the value of your company in relation to what you've spent on it to date. Your expenditure has nothing to do with the value of your company. Think only of its market value. Of course, this also means that if you've spent £1million in your company and no-one wants to buy it, the value of your company is easy to calculate—it's zero.

A useful way of getting some idea of the value of your company, assuming there is an interested buyer, is to estimate what could be paid in royalty payments over the life of your patent or for the number of years that your product is likely to be sold. This means estimating the likely end-user price of the product, sales throughout those years and how these are likely to be affected by competition. What you end up with is not at all accurate but at least it gives you an idea. An amount equal to or a reasonable percentage of this would not be a bad starting point for negotiations. It is advisable to enter negotiations in a non-adversarial way and aim for an agreement that is a win–win for both parties.

It is very likely that you formed your IPC because you're a person of many ideas and capable of many inventions. So, when the opportunity arises, sell one invention at a time—not your whole IPC. In any case, it's unlikely that a buyer would be interested in your many different inventions. However, in certain countries the tax regime may be such that it would be financially advantageous to have a separate IPC for each invention. Take advice from a tax lawyer in your country about this issue.

When you sell an invention from your IPC there will be implications in the transaction that you need to take into account. In the purchase agreement you may well be required to keep confidential any commercially sensitive intellectual property, e.g. know-how not revealed in your patent, or the business strategy that that company will adopt for your product. At worse, the agreement may restrict you from undertaking any research in the area of your invention that may be considered by the company to be competitive. Consider this requirement very seriously, it may severely restrict your ability to continue research in your area of expertise.

Having come this far, it could be that you decide against selling your IPC and choose to run the company as an innovation-driven enterprise with the objective of turning your invention into products that you then sell. You believe that your invention can be developed into a product, you have intellectual property (patent application or patent) to protect you from competitors, and you want to take your product all the way through to manufacture and sales. What will this involve?

Option 4: Manufacture and sell your invention through your start-up

Recently I was fortunate to have made email contact with a very successful entrepreneur, Gareth Williams—a mathematics graduate, a computer programmer and an ardent skier. While at Manchester University, frustrated by the hours spent searching different airline sites for convenient and cheap flights to ski resorts in France, Williams and two friends set up Skyscanner. Skyscanner is a search engine that compares flight, hotel and car hire prices across the world. Set up in 2001, Skyscanner was acquired by a Chinese travel company, Ctrip, for US$1.6 billion in 2016. It is one of a small number of UK companies to go from start-up to achieving a valuation of over US$1 billion. Asked what he thought would be the most helpful advice he could give anyone thinking of starting such a start-up company, these were his comments:

There is general start-up advice, and then there's advice that applies to scientists/academia. In relation to the latter, particularly from an academia point of view I would say…

- Learn lots. There is so much on the internet. Here's an example—http://a16z.com/2016/03/07/all-about-network-effects—the value of this for people thinking about a consumer product is amazing, and it's free.
- Sign up to interesting venture capital blogs (e.g. Brad Feld, Fred Wilson, Tom Tunguz). They share the information that entrepreneurs glean but don't have time to write about.
- A successful start-up is also about culture. Scientists and techies tend not to like to think about this as an explicit thing. But the way you behave will ripple down the ages within the company. So be choiceful.
- But the most important bit of advice I feel is this: https://sivers.org/multiply. In academia (and in youth) it's tempting to think it's ALL about the idea and that execution is just a detail. Not so!
- Tenacity is one of the defining principles of entrepreneurship.

With these words of advice in mind let's look at the steps necessary to give your new company the best chance of success. Among these are writing a business plan, putting together the management team, employing an experienced managing director (Chief Executive Officer), finding investors, and so on. But the first requirement for any business is not, as you might think, to develop your product (although we will talk about this later in the chapter). The first requirement is to determine that there are customers who are prepared to buy your eventual product. To determine whether you will have customers or not can be more difficult. Even so, it is important to make your best effort to find out who your customers will be. For this you will need to undertake market research.

Market research

Market research helps you to identify and understand the most important element of a successful business—the customer. Having a great product is not enough. Market research will tell you who your customers are (if any), what they want and when and what they're prepared to pay for it. Market research will also tell you who your competitors are and what you will have to do to get a share of the market. Remember also that you will need to show your market research to investors who might help fund your company to develop and launch your product.

Here is a note of caution. It is not uncommon for an inventor to believe that the product they create will be in such great demand that customers will beat a path to their door, 'so I don't need to do market research…'. Others don't do any market research because they don't want to hear any negative feedback and feel that it reflects on them personally. Resist this temptation; it is likely to be a big mistake. Market research done early enough can save you a lot of time and even money in the development of your product because what your customers tell you may well determine the shape, size and specification of the product you eventually launch.

You can choose to pay a market research company or you can do a great deal of the work yourself. There are two types of market research data to be gathered: primary and secondary. Primary market research means talking to potential customers directly, for instance in focus groups or perhaps using surveys. Secondary research, by contrast, is the sort of research you can do in the library, from your desk and on the internet. It involves gathering together as much information as you can about the sector you think your invention fits into and about competing products, companies and up-coming technology. It's a good idea to start by gathering your secondary data yourself, certainly before you consider paying a market research company to do your market research for you. Reference librarians in local and university libraries can be very knowledgeable and know their way around the business reference section. You can find a great deal of valuable data on the internet from organisations such as government agencies and trade associations, of which there are hundreds all offering different information. Some market research companies, consultants, and even some of their customers will publish some of their data online for free. The Office for National Statistics in the UK publish an annual survey of businesses. The Federation of Small Businesses and the British Chambers of Commerce are also worth exploring for online information.

There are five fundamental things that you need to find out from your market research:

1. Is there a market for your proposed novel product?
2. How big is the market for your product?
3. Who is going to buy your product—individuals? Businesses? Which individuals or businesses?
4. How much is your customer willing to pay for your product? How often?
5. Does the amount your customer will pay for your product make you any money?

Once you have established that your product does indeed offer you a significant business opportunity, you would be well advised to go into your market research in more detail as it is the detail that potential investors are likely to ask you about. Everyone will ask you what your USP is—your unique selling point. In other words, what makes your invention different from anything similar on the market? You will need to be able to succinctly explain to people who are not in your field what makes your invention different from other commercially available products. Take a careful look at what your potential customer currently has access to in order to realistically assess the competition. Then consider how likely it is that your potential customer will choose your product over what they can already have, and how the customers' buying behaviour might change in the future.

It's not only the customer whose needs will have to be considered, it may be worth thinking about whether retailers or distributors might have a logistics problem with your invention—will it need to be refrigerated/require a lot of storage space/need specialist handling etc? You also need to be aware of any future changes in legislation in the area of your invention that might affect your business.

You are almost certain to be asked whether you believe the sector in which your invention fits economically is growing or shrinking. You may want to familiarise yourself with the market trends, and you certainly want to keep an eye on other products that your competitors are bringing onto the market. Keep up to date on this and don't necessarily rely on information you find on the internet, it may be wildly out of date. You can buy market information and market intelligence online. Several well-known and reputable companies can provide you with market reports on your particular market sector. Before buying a report, however, have a good look through the press releases these companies publish on their websites as you may find the data you are looking for is already there for free.

So that is your secondary market research. What about primary market research? This is a bit trickier. There are two types of information anyone doing primary market research is looking for, quantitative and qualitative. Quantitative involves gathering statistics about what income bracket your potential customer will be in, or if you are supplying a business, what that business currently pays for the type of product you are developing. Qualitative involves finding out how people might feel about your proposed product.

It may seem very early in the life of your invention to be testing it out on potential customers. However, asking a few people a few careful questions could stop you from going down a dead-end if your potential customer really doesn't like the idea of something that you are doing. Here's an example. There are many reasons for determining the various components of arterial blood, particularly non-invasively. You can get very close to arterial blood on the inside of the eyelid where arterial blood is just a few molecular layers away. But do patients like having a device, no matter how small, placed under their eyelid? In my experience, they do not. So, no matter how good a site the inner eyelid may be for monitoring all sorts of useful parameters, the customer is likely to reject a product that needs to be placed under the eyelid.

You can't just go out on the street, collar passers-by and start firing questions at them—for a start, you need a licence from your local authority. You also need to have a very clear idea of what information you want to get out of your primary market research before you speak to anyone at all. To be blunt, what you need is the type of affirmation from your audience that would be reassuring to an investor. It has to be impartial so there is no point in gathering biased information and for this reason you might want to consider involving a third party. This could be a market research agency but bear in mind that many market research agencies don't take on small projects, say costing below a few thousand pounds. A freelance market researcher, however, may be happy to help you. You don't have to do all of your primary research at once, of course, you will be continuing to get opinions on your invention as you work towards turning it into a product.

Online survey companies such as SurveyMonkey can be a useful resource, depending on your invention, especially if you need a bit of free guidance about putting together a questionnaire. Be wary, though, whenever you're working online as the information you inadvertently give away in a survey could be commercially sensitive and helpful to a competitor. You could also take a look at some of the big-name polling companies, such as YouGov. These polling companies publish a great deal of information for free online. It is always worth having a look through the press releases and reports they publish on their websites to get a feel for what the general public are saying about a particular market sector. Another particularly useful source of information for small businesses is the British Library Business and IP Centre.

To begin with, though, you might try gathering a few people together, for instance friends and family of work colleagues, and form a focus group. You probably don't even need to have a prototype of your invention, you could show them drawings or describe the idea and get them to discuss it. Make sure that the people you ask to join your focus group are not just people you think are going to think favourably towards your invention. Also, try to make sure the group is as diverse as you can make it.

I remember a situation a few years ago when our research group had successfully developed a patient monitoring instrument for use in an Intensive Care Unit. We needed some advice on the design of the monitor so we asked a nurse working in the unit. Straight away she said 'make it small enough to be carried in one hand so that I can open swing doors with the other hand'. That wasn't quite what we expected, but we considered the suggestion anyway. We decided to work on designing a monitor that was battery powered and portable, small and light enough to be carried in one hand. We received an order for over 100 of these monitors from a major company within two months of showing the instrument at an invited presentation. There are, unfortunately, not many situations in life where a survey of one turns out so successfully!

Timescales

It is vitally important to be realistic about the time it will take to progress your invention from proof-of-principle to product launch. This is not meant to put you off the idea of starting a company, but inventors often badly underestimate the time required to launch a product and this can result in the company running out of money. If you don't have a good idea of how long it will take to develop your invention into a product it will turn your business plan into guesswork.

Timescales for product development can be highly variable. The idea of a hybrid car was first conceived as early as 1900 and the electric car at about the same time. Yet it was not until the 1990s that these vehicles were seen on the roads in any significant numbers—a gestation period of over 90 years! The fuel cell car was first thought of in around 1960 and has yet to reach product stage. Similarly, wearable computers were conceived in 1995 but have only just made it to the market. At the other extreme, the time from invention to product for the smartphone was less than 5 years with take-off occurring very quickly afterwards.

What is useful in this regard is the approach used by NASA. NASA have created a system by which they describe the nine stages they go through in the development of a new product. NASA call their nine stages technology readiness levels (TRLs). This system of TRLs was used in NASA's missions throughout the 1990s (John C Mankins (1995), http://www.hq.nasa.gov/office/codeq/trl/trl.pdf). By applying a timescale to each level you can give yourself an idea of how long it will take you to get from invention to product. This is how the timescale for the development of your invention might look.

BOX 3.1
Technology Readiness Levels

NASA employs a technology readiness level (TRL) process to assess the flight readiness of a given technology under development on the basis of its level of maturity (see Appendix D in this report). The TRL is rated on a scale of 1 to 9 depending on the degree of concept development, analytic and empirical validation, and ultimately, flight validation (see Figure 3.1.1).

TRL 9: Actual system "flight proven" through successful mission operations

TRL 8: Actual system completed and "flight qualified" through test and demonstration (ground or space)

TRL 7: System prototype demonstration in a space environment

TRL 6: System/subsystem model or prototype demonstration in a relevant environment (ground or space)

TRL 5: Component and/or breadboard validation in relevant environment

TRL 4: Component and/or breadboard validation in laboratory environment

TRL 3: Analytical and experimental critical formula and/or characteristic proof-of-concept

TRL 2: Technology concept and/or application formulated

TRL 1: Basic principle observed and reported

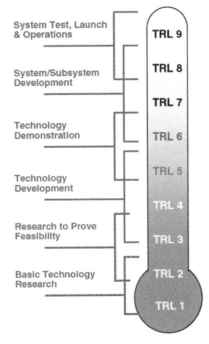

FIGURE 3.1.1 Technology readiness level scale.
SOURCE: Courtesy of NASA.

SOURCE: NASA In-Space Propulsion Web site at http://www.grc.nasa.gov/WWW/InSpace/when.html.

TRL 1

Level 1 is where you realise that your idea could be translated into an invention.

TRL 2

Level 2 involves working out how to turn your idea into an invention. This is when you should begin to write the *specification* of your product. Your 'spec' will be constantly added to and updated by your development team all the way through the development of your product and provides a history of the stages the finished product has gone through.

TRL 3

Level 3 is when you establish proof-of-principle using something like a 'breadboard' layout of your device (invention). This is also when work should begin on market research alongside further developing your technology.

TRL 4

At Level 4 you are looking to validate what you established as your proof-of-principle while continuing your market research. The end-user price of your product will, to a large extent, determine the specification and the design of the product from here on. Keep firmly in mind during the development of your product that there is a limit to what the customer will pay for the product.

TRL 5

It is at this stage that you need to consider how you will manage the development from here if your invention needs to be compatible with a product or system that is already in existence. This development will continue through TRL 6 and 7.

TRL 6

By the end of Level 5 you should have something that you can demonstrate. During Level 6 you test this demonstrable product in the environment it is designed to be used in and make appropriate changes as necessary.

TRL 7

Level 7 is when you fine-tune the prototype until you have something as close as possible to the product you wish to manufacture.

TRL 8

Level 8 is your last chance to make any technological changes.

TRL 9

Level 9 is where you iron out the last of the bugs or difficulties before proceeding towards a pre-production run.

Note: Your *specification* includes not only technical performance requirements but will also take account of regulatory requirements in terms of product exterior design, materials and electromagnetic compatibility and emissions, fire-resistance and electrical insulation compliance. These vary from country to country.

The valley of death

Many small companies fail because they are unable to progress from TRL 3 to TRL 7 because they descend into what is commonly called 'the valley of death' and never emerge. So, you can see that the critical period in the development of a company is the time between the successful development of a basic prototype and the point at which the product can be manufactured. It is said that for every product that succeeds, hundreds get left behind in the valley of death (see figure 3.1).

Why should this be so? There are many reasons, but what often happens is that research funding or government grants enable scientists to create a proof-of-principle prototype. But there the funding ends. Investors, business angels, entrepreneurs and banks are often willing to provide loans or investment for manufacture but are not willing to provide finance for technological development that is at an earlier stage because it is considered high risk. This situation was described by James Darcy in his article 'Navigating the valley of death' [1]. He says: 'In fact, the valley of death could be viewed as an inevitable feature of the way that many capitalist societies are structured. Industry tends to invest in products that are far along the innovation spectrum due to the lower perceived risk, while fundamental research is by-and-large supported by government money. The bit in the middle, (TRL 4, 5 and 6) where science is translated into commercial products, tends to miss out on the cash.'

The valley of death is probably more risky for creative scientists than for other innovators. The inventions of creative scientists tend to be at the cutting-edge of technology. The cutting-edge nature of these innovations means that it can take a long time to create a manufacturable product out of a basic prototype because the

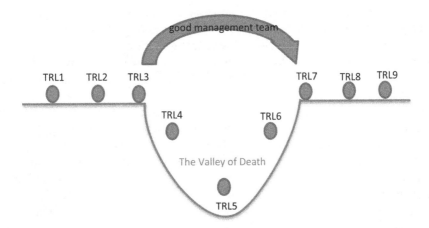

Figure 3.1. The valley of death.

invention can be more complicated than first thought. An invention, in concept, might be brilliant but the technology may not be available which would turn it into a manufactured product with the right volume, cost and performance specification. Mobile phones, for instance, did not really take off until they were small enough to be convenient and were at the right price for people to buy for personal use. Sometimes an invention is so far ahead of its time that there is no market for it. The perceived wisdom in marketing is that for a product to be successful it has to meet a need, it has to have 'market pull' rather than 'technology push'. But it is debateable if this applies to the cutting-edge inventions that creative scientists are often involved with. An invention may address a need that still has to be created. As Jesko von Windheim puts it [2]: 'Technology translation, in other words, isn't just a "two body" problem of "finding a need" and "filling a need." It's a nonlinear, multi-dimensional problem, where the market is often a *function* of the innovation.' This is another reason why the valley of death is a more formidable challenge if you are a creative scientist.

What is typical of the companies that make it through the valley of death is that they not only have innovators, they also have a good management team of experienced business people and engineers. They have a knowledge of their product and an understanding of their market. It is therefore not surprising that it is often said that a moderately good idea with good management is more likely to succeed than a brilliant idea with poor management.

Timescale for a product—an example

Timescales for product development vary a great deal from product to product in different industry sectors. Software products have a much faster timeline (6 months to a year) while medical products can take up to 10 years. The important point is to recognize that there are many tasks that need to be done to take an invention to market. You have to be time-competitive in accomplishing all the tasks because your competitors may also be working on similar products and you need to be the first to bring the product to market to create an entry barrier for competitors.

Here is an actual example of the time involved in taking an invention through the necessary stages to product launch. A few years ago, one of us (SR) invented a novel windscreen washer nozzle. This washer nozzle is now used in over 80% of the vehicles currently on the road in the United States and is also used in many models in Europe (figure 3.2).

The basic invention was the realisation that the instability of two jets in a cavity could produce an oscillating flow field, as shown in the patent drawing (figure 3.3).

So how was the basic invention transformed into the final product? To give you an idea, the following were a few of the considerations in the development of the invention into the final product.

- The early version of the invention was a large device, too large for use on a car. We needed to see if the idea would work in a smaller device because the physics of the problem could change at a smaller scale due to pronounced viscosity effects of the washer fluid.

Figure 3.2. Two windscreen nozzles on the bonnet of a car.

- We had to ensure that the jets could oscillate at the required amplitude, the required flow rates and at a range of temperatures. The variation in the viscosity of the water with temperature was a big factor in this consideration.
- The entire device had to be packaged into a 'standard' housing to fit on car bonnets (hoods). This was a challenge and the basic invention had to be 'tweaked' quite a bit to conform to the required footprint of the exterior housing.
- We had to ensure that these could be economically manufactured using injection moulding. This meant that the device performance could not be sensitive to geometric changes within the maximum tolerances of critical dimensions related to fluid flow paths in the device. Methods other than injection moulding were not cost-effective.
- We had to ensure that this washer nozzle would perform satisfactorily with the standard available washer pump located in the engine compartment of motor vehicles.

These requirements are included, along with many others, in the timeline shown in figure 3.4. The timeline gives an idea of how the invention progressed to product stage, but remember that as well as dealing with the technology aspects of any product development you will, in parallel, have to manage the administration and

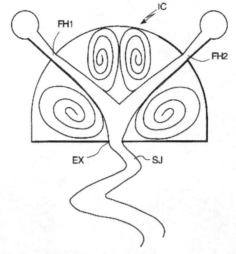

Figure 3.3. Detail of the windscreen nozzle.

financial aspects of the company. These have not been included in the timeline. The windscreen nozzle took three years between the initial invention (TLR 1) to the launch of the product (TLR 9). This might be a good example of the timescale involved in the development of a product but be aware that it is nevertheless quite a short timescale for this type of product.

With a realistic view of the timescale for product development and all the other issues we have considered, you should now be ready to consider starting your company.

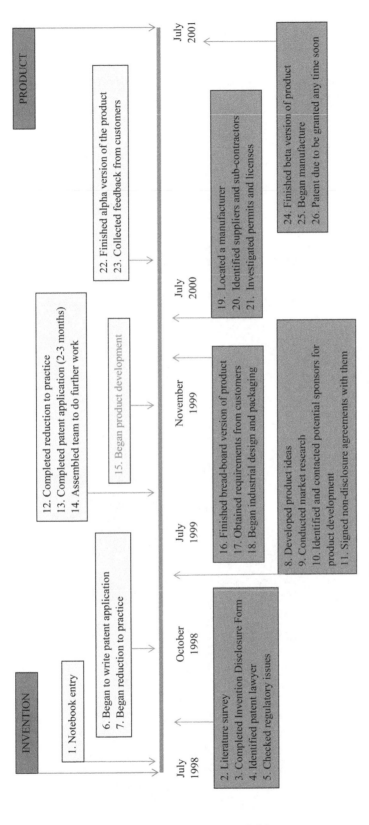

Figure 3.4. Invention-to-product timescale windscreen washer nozzle.

References

[1] Darcy J 2014 Navigating the valley of death *Phys. World* **27** 11 November 2014
[2] von Windheim J 2014 More push than pull *Phys. World* **27** 11, November 2014

Chapter 4

A start-up—formalities

You are now in possession of some information about your customer and you have timescales to product launch. What sort of company would you like to start?

You can start a business by setting up on your own. There are various names for this around the world, for instance in India you would be a sole proprietor, in France an enterprise individuelle, and in the United States or the UK a sole trader. Nevertheless, no matter where in the world you are, you will need to register your business so that it has legal status, and always get good tax advice.

Sole trader

For our purposes here we will call this type of business a 'sole trader'. A sole trader is the sole owner of their business and is entirely responsible for its success or failure. As such, a sole trader is entitled to all the profit that the business makes but on the other hand has unlimited liability. This means that should your business find itself in debt, you, the owner, will be liable for the debt. If the business is declared bankrupt, your personal assets are at stake. Also, if a customer sues your business they are, in fact, suing you—in most countries the law regards a sole trader and their business as one entity. The burden of unlimited liability is a disincentive for many scientists.

The main advantage of running a business as a sole trader is that you have full control of your business. There is less paperwork involved in registering yourself as a sole trader than as a company so you could start your business straight away. Also, generally, accountants will charge less for preparing sole trader annual accounts because there is less work involved. If your invention was developed by a team of researchers, a business founded on it would most likely have more than one owner, i.e. it could not be a 'sole trader' business.

A company

Any company you start is a legal entity. There are, however, many types of these legal entities available to the scientist depending on where in the world you happen to be. The type of company you should be looking to start is one where the company is separate from the people who own the company (shareholders)—for example, you—or from those who run the company (directors). This type of company is a legal entity separate from its owners and will exist beyond the life of its members. It means that your liabilities are limited—look for the word 'limited' in the name of the type of company you wish to start. If you have created your invention as part of a group then all of you would have a stake in the company, but the company should still be able to exist without you or any of your fellow directors or shareholders should any of you be unable or unwilling to continue working within it.

New proposed EU legislation, the European Private Company Statute, is good news for entrepreneurs. It will enable a European Private Company—an SPE—to be formed. This proposal will enable entrepreneurs to set up their business in the form of an SPE which will be subject to the same company law throughout all member states of the EU. This will have the advantage that an SPE can be set up instead of, for example, setting up a 'GmbH' in Germany and an 'SAS' in France. An SPE will save time and reduce the legal costs associated with forming a company in different member states of the EU. It will also allow the transfer of the domicile of a company from one EU member state to another. At the time of writing, the date for the implementation of the SPE is not known.

In the meantime, if you wish to start a company in the EU you will need to find out about the types of company available to you in your country. For instance, in France you could start an SAS (*société par actions simplifiée*) which is a limited liability company, or an SARL (*société á responsibilité*) which is a company limited by shares.

In India there are an array of business types that can be formed ranging from Partnership to Limited Liability Partnership to Public Sector Enterprises listed on stock exchanges. The Private Limited Company, Pvt Ltd is probably closest to the UK Ltd (see below) and could well be the choice for scientists in India. Shares in a Pvt Ltd are held privately and cannot be offered to the public.

In Nigeria, a private company limited by shares is designated an 'Ltd', whereas a non-profit company limited by guarantee is an 'Ltd/Gte'.

As you would expect, the actual formation of companies is different from country to country. In the United States, for example, it is the individual states that incorporate most businesses and not the federal government. The business type in the United States that is commonly the choice of inventors is a Limited Liability Company, an LLC, whose owners have limited liability. This means that if the business owes money or faces a lawsuit, only the assets of the business are at risk. The personal assets of the owners of the LLC are protected. LLC owners report their business profits or losses on their personal income tax.

Of course, wherever you are, the prudent way of forming your company is to take advice from an accountant or of the government authority responsible for company formations.

Private limited companies

If we take the UK as an example, a scientist is very likely to start a private limited company (Ltd). This can be either a private company limited by shares, usually called a private limited company, or a private company limited by guarantee. Most start-up companies are private limited companies. A private limited company is a flexible legal entity that can be adapted to fit the requirements of the individuals starting the company. It can vary from a small family company to the subsidiary of a large group but still be a trading entity in its own right.

A private company limited by shares is owned by its members—the shareholders. Each shareholder is liable for the original value of the shares they were issued *but did not pay for*. For example, take a shareholder who was allocated 500 shares valued at £1 each. The shareholder was required to pay £1 each for 100 of these shares. If the company fails, the shareholder will be liable only to the value of the shares that he or she did not pay for, i.e. £400. (www.gov.uk/limited-company-formation.) In this way a shareholder's personal assets are protected in the event of the company's insolvency. Of course, the money invested in the company will be lost.

So, the obvious advantage of a private company limited by shares is that the company's shareholders will be liable for any company debt only up to the level of their own investment in the company and no more.

The other type of private limited company is a private company limited by guarantee. This means that the members of the company financially support it to an agreed amount. These guarantors are members (not shareholders) who agree to make a limited contribution towards the payment of the company's debts in the event of the assets of the company falling short of its debts. Social enterprises and 'not-for-profit' organisations are usually registered in this manner.

Some of the disadvantages associated with limited liability companies are that they have to submit annual accounts which can be time-consuming and relatively costly. Also, limited liability companies cannot raise capital by publicly selling company shares in the way that public liability companies (Plcs) are able to do. This means that if you wish at any time to sell some of your shares in a private limited company to raise funds for example, you cannot do this by offering the sale of your shares to the public. Public liability companies can, and do, do this all the time. Your only option is to sell your shares to family members or friends but even in this regard you need to take advice from an accountant.

In general, the advantages of a limited liability company outweigh the disadvantages and this is why they are the preferred company type for the majority of start-up businesses.

Social entrepreneurship

The entrepreneurs we have described up to this point in this book are innovators who have the personality and skills to bring new products or services to market. Entrepreneurs who are successful in coping with the risks of a start-up benefit from the profits of the company. Those who fail suffer losses and, in certain situations, a loss of credibility.

Social entrepreneurship on the other hand is about implementing solutions to social, environmental or cultural problems. Business entrepreneurs assess their performance in terms of revenues, profits or share price, social entrepreneurs view their performance in terms of their returns to society. Even so, while the goal of the social entrepreneur is not about profit, they still have to be financially astute to remain sustainable.

However, while business entrepreneurs strive to make a profit, the profit motive and benefit to society are, of course, not exclusive. In his book *The Wealth of Nations*, Adam Smith argues that 'it is not from the benevolence of the butcher, the brewer, or the baker that we expect our dinner, but from their regard to their own self-interest'. His view was that when individuals pursue their own interests their decisions can result in benefit to others.

Whether you are a social entrepreneur or a business entrepreneur there is high regard from most people for the accomplishments of both. Outstanding examples are Muhammad Yunus, the father of microcredit, and Steve Jobs whose successes at creating financial services and brilliant new products, respectively, contribute greatly to improving the lives of millions.

One of the earliest social entrepreneurs was Florence Nightingale, the 'lady with the lamp' who in 1854 initiated the nursing of sick and wounded soldiers during the Crimean War. In 1860 she established the Nightingale Training School at St Thomas' Hospital, London, the first professional training school for nurses. She also played a significant role in the founding of the International Red Cross. What Florence Nightingale did was change society for the better, an inspiring social entrepreneur.

A more recent luminary is the Bangladeshi social entrepreneur Professor Mohammad Yunus who is well known for initiating the concept of microfinance and microcredit. In 1983 he founded the Grameen Bank which pioneered the concept of supporting millions of people in rural communities with small loans in developing countries in Asia, Africa and Latin America. In 2006 Professor Yunus was awarded the Nobel Peace Prize for his work.

Social entrepreneurs, like other entrepreneurs, have a vision of what they want to achieve and make it happen. They thrive on change. But if social entrepreneurs want to change society they have to be trustworthy and pay a high regard for ethical business practices. Unlike other entrepreneurs, social entrepreneurs often don't have the skills needed to implement their visions but they do know how to build a team around them that can execute their ideas. In social entrepreneurship it is often easier for the idea to attract a skilful team of like-minded people than might be the case in a for-profit start-up. Social entrepreneurs are more often than not motivated by emotion where the desire to change society for the better is their *raison d'être*.

Also, social entrepreneurs are driven to tackle often unidentified problems such as future food and water shortages and over-population. This is quite unlike other entrepreneurs where the focus is on current market opportunities. Social entrepreneurs, therefore, find it much more difficult to raise funds because investors see their organisations as much riskier than entrepreneurial businesses with well-researched markets.

This lack of investors leads to a further problem encountered by social entrepreneurs—the salary gap between social and other businesses. Social entrepreneurs and employers often have to endure low or non-existent salaries so that these organisations, not surprisingly, struggle to retain qualified staff which is, of course, a serious disadvantage. The irony in this is that while social entrepreneurs see themselves as addressing crucial social issues they are often confronted by disinterest by the society they seek to support.

Social entrepreneurs also have to tackle the dilemma that the people they help are those least able to pay for it. Business entrepreneurship is based on trade, the exchange of money for goods or services, but social enterprises have to find other resources to remain sustainable.

More recently the internet and social media have provided social entrepreneurs with a variety of resources from like-minded people around the world. These websites enable social entrepreneurs to spread their ideas worldwide and so attract potential investors, donors or volunteers. Another favourable development is open source software programs the source code of which is available to anyone for free. Such software is usually the result of collaboration among individuals from around the world. In the same way, open source technology enables people to collaborate and solve local problems. By these means social entrepreneurs are able to achieve their goals from home with no need for office space or start-up capital.

So, are social entrepreneurs the same as philanthropists? No, not strictly speaking. Social entrepreneurs seek economic and social benefits for others by giving away money but in a controlled way so that they can influence how the money is spent. Philanthropists may also do the same but the organisational structures they set up may allow them to retain control of the use of the funds and there may in certain circumstances be tax advantages as well.

But, whether a business entrepreneur or a social entrepreneur, your organisation still has to be profitable to be sustainable so read on. This book is intended to help you do just that.

Setting up a private limited company

The requirements for setting up a company vary from country to country. So to give you some idea of what is required we will take the formation of a company in the UK as an example. At least it will give you some idea of what is involved in starting a company no matter where your company might be located. All the requirements mentioned here for setting up a private limited company in the UK are detailed on the very useful gov.uk website.

When you form your company in the UK the process is described as 'the incorporation' of your business and is also referred to as 'the company registration.' In the UK all limited companies must be registered (incorporated) with Companies House. Before you go ahead and register your company you will need:

1. a company name and address;
2. company director(s);
3. the allocation of shares to each shareholder and the names and addresses of the shareholders;
4. memorandum of association and articles of association;
5. to have set up your company for Corporation Tax.

1. Company name and address

   If you don't have specific business premises then use your own address. You then need to choose a name for your company. Do a search for free with gov.uk or any number of other websites that offer the same service to see if the name you'd like is available. If it is, check if it is also available in any other countries you might want to expand into later. You should also search for availability of a domain name to match your trading name as you will need to have an online presence, especially if you intend to do any sales or marketing of your product online. Registering your company name, which is part of registering a private limited company, protects the name from the date of registration even though the company is not legally required to begin trading from that date.

2. Company directors

   Your company must have at least one director. Another company can be a director of your company, but at least one of the directors of your company must be a person. A director is legally bound to try to make their company a success, to make decisions for the benefit of the company only and to follow the company's rules as shown in its articles of association (see more later). A director is also responsible for keeping company records, for reporting changes such as new shareholdings or new directors to the responsible authorities in your particular country. (In the UK such reports are sent to Companies House and HM Revenue and Customs) and to make sure that the company's accounts reflect the business of the company fairly.

   A company can hire, for instance, an accountant, to manage these tasks but the director(s) will still be legally responsible for the company's records, accounts and performance.

3. Shares and shareholders

   (see http://www.gov.uk/limited-company-formations/shareholders)

   A company limited by shares must have at least one shareholder who can be a director. The number of shareholders is unlimited. The shareholders are the owners of the company and have voting rights so that they can vote and agree to changes to the company.

   When registering your company, you'll need to make a 'statement of capital' which is a document that provides the information about the issued shares in a company at a particular time. It should include:

   - the number of shares of each type the company has and their total value;
   - the names and addresses of all the shareholders.

   As an example, a company that issues 1000 shares at £1 each has a share capital, i.e. an aggregate nominal value, of £1000.

   When registering your company, your statement of capital should also contain information about shares known as 'prescribed particulars'. These state what rights each type ('class') of share gives the shareholder. The information should include:

- the share of dividends the shareholder will get;
- whether the shares can be redeemed. i.e. exchanged for money by the shareholder;
- whether these shares give the shareholder the right to vote on certain company matters;
- how many votes these shares give the shareholder.

4. Memorandum of association and articles of association

The memorandum of association of a company describes the structure of the company and is the document that defines the relationship between the company, its investors and the general public. It is one of the documents required to incorporate a company in many countries such as the United Kingdom, Ireland and India and other member countries of the Commonwealth. The memorandum of association is a legal document which cannot be changed before or after incorporation of the company.

The articles of association of a company are the regulations which set out the rules by which a company runs its internal affairs. Articles of association are a requirement for the formation of a company in many countries like the United Kingdom, India, etc. The memorandum of association and the articles of association together form the constitution of a company. The equivalent requirement in the United States is articles of incorporation.

5. Corporation tax

Apart from knowing a little about what corporation tax is, this is a matter that will be dealt with by your accountant. When you form your company you will be required to register your company for corporation tax with the relevant authority in your country. Again, your accountant will do this.

Many countries impose corporation tax generally on the net profits of a company. The rate of tax varies from country to country. In some countries such as the United States, Canada, Germany, Japan and Switzerland, corporation tax can also be imposed at sub-country level by states, provinces, cantons, cities, etc.

Corporation tax rates vary widely, varying (as I write this in 2018) from 12.5% in Ireland, 11% to 15% in Canada (Federal), 16.5% in Hong Kong, and 28% in New Zealand. In the United States corporation tax can vary from 15% to 35% (federal) with taxes in individual states varying from 0% to 10% deductible in calculating federal taxable income.

So let's hope that it won't be too long before your company starts generating profits—and so making you eligible for corporation tax!

Registering your company

Before you can start your business you need to register (or incorporate) your company. Generally what is required is the name and address of the company, the name of at least one director and one shareholder, the articles of association and setting the company up for corporation tax. The details of how to register your company, as you might expect, vary from country to country. However, in most countries you have a choice: you can register directly with the relevant authority in your country (for instance, in the UK this is Companies House); through a company formations agent; or ask an accountant to do it for you. The latter, of course, will come with professional advice and is likely to be the costlier option.

A guide to registering a company in many countries can be found at www.icaew.com.

There are companies in the UK who will set up your company for you online for £7–100, depending on your needs. See, for example, www.theformationscompany. com or www.yourcompanyformations.co.uk but there are many to choose from.

Shares, dilution and valuation

Soon after registering your company you will find that the company will no doubt need cash. Let's assume that in the beginning the founders provide this as loans to the company. But before too long you'll need more money and this will lead you to fund-raising (more about this later). Assuming that this is successful, how do you now calculate the shareholding of each shareholder in the company? Here is a simple example to illustrate what to do.

Assume that your company is a private company limited by shares and had originally issued a total of 1000 shares at £1 each. Founders A, B and C were allocated 600, 200 and 200 shares each and in their judgement (mainly guesswork) the company is valued at £100 000. (This figure is based entirely on what they believe the company is worth. This, by no means, reflects that this is what the company can be sold for!) See table 4.1. A and B then invest £10 000 and £5000, respectively, in the company which equates to 100 and 50 additional shares for A and B.

Table 4.2 shows the conversion of this new investment into shares. As you can see, A's number of shares increases from 600 to 700 and B's from 200 to 250 with their percentage shareholding now 61% and 22%. C's shareholding has decreased from 20% to 17%. The post-investment valuation (post-money valuation) of the company has increased from £100 000 to £115 000. The company's shares now total 1150.

Table 4.1. Year 1 shareholding.

Year 1 £100k Valuation Share and loan structure Company valuation	Shareholders	Shareholder's no. of shares	Shareholding %
	A	600	60%
	B	200	20%
	C	200	20%
	others		
£100 000		**1000**	**100%**

A year later, as a result of success in the development of its product the Board values the company at £250 000. It now raises £50 000 from a single, new investor. The number of shares issued and given to the investor is:

$$\text{number of new shares issued} = \frac{50\,000}{250\,000} \times 1150 = 230$$

So the total number of shares that has been issued by the company is now 1380. The shareholdings of A, B and C are shown in table 4.3.

So you can see that the founders' shareholdings have dropped from 61%, 22% and 17% to 51%, 18% and 15%, respectively. They nevertheless have £50 000 to invest and grow the company, and the valuation of the company is now £300 000.

Let's take another example. Say two founders, A and B, start a company, authorise 1000 shares and issue themselves 500 shares each. So they each own 50% of the company.

Next, they raise £50 000 from an investor who wants 20% of the company. How many additional shares do they have to issue in exchange for the £50 000? Simple. If the number of shares is x,

$$\text{then } \frac{x}{1000 + x} = \frac{1}{5}$$

so $x = 250$

Table 4.2. Shareholding after round 1 investment.

Conversion into share capital Shareholders	Investment	Additional shares issued	Shareholder's no. of shares	New shareholding%	Company valuation
A	£10 000	100	700	61%	
B	£5000	50	250	22%	
C			200	17%	
others					
			1150	100%	£115 000

Table 4.3. Shareholding after round 2 investment.

Year 2 New fund raising Shareholders	New investment	Additional shares issued	New no. of shares	New shareholding %	New company valuation
A			700	51%	
B			250	18%	
C			200	14%	
others	£50 000	230	230	17%	
			1380	100%	£300 000

Note: Although the shareholding of the three original Founders has diluted from 100% to 84%, their aggregate share value has increased from £115 000 to £252 000. It is common for further rounds of shares to be issued before the eventual sale or exit of the business is achieved.

The total number of shares issued now is 1250.

$$A \text{ has } \frac{500}{1250} \quad 40\%$$

$$B \text{ has } \frac{500}{1250} \quad 40\%$$

$$\text{Investor 1 has } \frac{250}{1250} \quad 20\%$$

So, the founders now each own 40% of the company, down from 50% but the company for the first time has money in the bank, i.e. £50 000, for developing the business which is probably much more valuable than the 20% shareholding that the founders have given up.

Next, assume that the company makes good progress with the development of its innovative products and its valuation has increased significantly. A new investor offers the company £200 000 for 20% of the company, which they accept. The number of shares given to the investor is, as calculated before, 313.

Total shares issued: 1250 + 313 = 1563

$$A \text{ has } \frac{500}{1563} \quad 32\%$$

$$B \text{ has } \frac{500}{1563} \quad 32\%$$

$$\text{Investor 1 has } \frac{250}{1563} \quad 16\%$$

$$\text{Investor 2 has } \frac{313}{1563} \quad 20\%$$

Again the founders and Investor 1 have seen their shareholdings in the company decrease. On the other hand, they have the comfort of £200 000 in working capital to boost their business. So, the point of all this is that while your percentage shareholding in your company may decrease, the value of the company, like an expanding pie, can get bigger and bigger so you can end up with a smaller percentage of a larger pie! Not surprisingly it is often repeated that 'it is better to own 1% of a billion-pound company than 100% of a worthless one'. This is worth remembering when raising funds for your start-up.

As a very simple further example about the value of a company, if you own the 100 issued shares in your company, i.e. 100% equity, and you are fortunate enough to find an investor who is prepared to offer you £10 000 for 20 new shares, then at least on this occasion you can say that the value of your company is:

$$\frac{120}{20} \times £10\ 000 = £60\ 000$$

Apart from this rare occurrence, the value of your company is what investors will accept rather than what you think it might be!

Now that you know what type of company you want to start, how to register the company, who your directors and other members of staff will be and how to allocate shares in your company, you're ready for the next big task—working out the business strategy for your company. We will get on to this in chapter 6, but in the meantime we need to address the issue of patents.

This chapter contains public sector information licensed under the Open Government Licence v3.0.

Chapter 5

Patenting your invention

So far we have avoided going into detail about patenting your invention. It is a complex and often time-consuming process best done by a patent attorney. However, there are things you can do before you even approach a patent attorney which can help to make the process a little smoother and can help to cut the costs.

The earliest known UK patent was granted in 1449 by Henry VI to a glass maker called John of Utynam. It granted the glass maker a 20-year monopoly on using a glass-making process that was not known to English glass makers. The condition of the grant was that, during the period of the patent, he taught the patented process to English glass makers. This is the function of a patent—to give the patent holder exclusive possession of or control over the use of or supply of their invention, while at the same time disclosing the information contained within the patent. This is why patents are published.

Patents are a form of intellectual property (IP). Other forms of intellectual property are trademarks, trade names, and copyright. Patents are often the form of intellectual property held by start-up companies whose businesses are built on protected inventions. A patent is often the principal asset in an innovation-driven enterprise. A patent has value.

According to a study by the US Department of Commerce, the revenues of intellectual property-intensive industries accounted for 35% of US GDP in 2010, of which about one third was revenue generated from patents, most of this either from the sale of the intellectual property or in royalty income. In 2010 this was worth nearly $2 trillion. It is estimated that over 80% of the market value of the Standard & Poor (S&P) 500 companies in the world today is based on their intangible assets—including patents, designs, trademarks and copyrights.

Patenting an invention is a time-consuming and lengthy process and can be costly. However, as your patent may well turn out to be the main asset in your start-up company, and it may be the thing that turns your invention into something saleable, it is important to get to grips with what a patent is and the process of obtaining patent protection for your invention.

doi:10.1088/978-0-7503-1146-5ch5

What is a patent?

Let's take an overview before we get into the details. A patent is a monopoly right granted by a country to an inventor to exclude others from making, using, selling (including importing and exporting) or holding in stock products based on the claimed invention in the patent, in exchange for the public disclosure of your invention. In other words, you are given the right to stop other people from commercialising your invention without your consent for the duration of the patent, in exchange for which your patent is published so that you reveal to the public what your invention is.

When you are granted a patent in your own country, you can apply for the patent to be granted in the other countries you would like to have a monopoly right in. As a general rule, this means you will be seeking patent protection in each of the countries where you intend to commercialise (and sell) your invention. Your patent will be examined in each of these countries by the patent examining authority and will be granted—or refused. In most cases the life of a patent is limited to 20 years from the date the patent was granted.

There is a further point to note. A patent is an exclusive right that allows the patent holder to prevent others from using an invention without the patent holder's consent. However, a patent does not necessarily give you the right to go ahead and commercialise your invention. In order to commercialise your invention, you will need to determine whether you have what is called 'the freedom to operate'. How can this be? Well, it could be that in order for you to commercialise your invention you need to incorporate into it aspects of someone else's invention—which they have patented. In this situation you do not have the freedom to operate. What you will require is a licence from the other inventor (or patent owner) before you can commercialise your own invention. So it is prudent to determine at an early stage in the patent process whether you have the freedom to operate or not. Your patent agent or lawyer will assess this for you.

However, in these circumstances you only need a licence in the countries where your product is going to be commercialised, used, or sold. If, for instance, their patent had been granted in Japan—but nowhere else—and you want to incorporate it into your own product for commercialisation and sale in the UK—and not in Japan—you will not need a licence to use their invention in the UK.

What is 'patentable'?

Not all inventions are patentable. In the UK, for instance, amongst other things you cannot patent discoveries (natural phenomena), surgical procedures, business methods, rules for playing games, or computer software. The list varies from country to country so you should always consult a patent attorney (or patent agent) for precise guidance on whether what you have invented is, in fact, patentable and where.

What are the conditions that need to be satisfied for an invention to be patentable? The requirements, according to European Patent law and most patent protection jurisdictions, are that the invention must:

- Be novel

    The invention must be novel, i.e. it must be new compared with what was known before the date that your patent application was filed. It must be distinguishable from all 'prior art'. Prior art refers not only to earlier inventions and products but also scientific and technical information that existed before the date of a patent application. It includes any public documents such as patents, technical publications, scientific journals, conference papers, marketing brochures, products, devices, equipment, processes and materials.

- Have an inventive step

    In order for an invention to be patentable, it must not only be different from the prior art, it has to involve an 'inventive step'. An inventive step is one that is not obvious 'to a person of ordinary skill in the art'. In other words, when the invention is compared to the prior art, the invention could not have been deduced from the prior art by a person skilled in the field of technology used in the invention.

- Have an industrial application

    The third requirement of patentability is that the claimed invention needs to be usable. The invention needs to be able to result in a product or service in a practical way.

Before filing a patent application

The cost of going to a patent attorney (lawyer or agent) and working with them to file a patent application, plus the subsequent filings (we'll go into this later), can seem high when you are just starting out. It is a really good idea to keep costs down by doing as much of the background research about your invention as you can yourself. To determine if your invention is novel, a literature and patent search should be undertaken. The literature search you can do yourself online. Obviously, such a search would start with a keyword search followed by a search for the core of the invention and its essential features.

The following databases may be helpful. Some require a subscription fee or payment per item:

- Google Scholar

    Free

    http://scholar.google.co.uk

- Pubmed

    For medical publications

    http://www.ncbi.nlm.nih.gov/pubmed

- Science Direct

    World's science, technology and medicine bibliographic and full-text data. Elsevier journals only.

http://www.sciencedirect.com/
- Web of Science
  Research journal bibliographic and full-text data. Requires access through an institution.
  http://thomsonreuters.com/thomson-reuters-web-of-science/

If you don't find anything which would question the novelty of the invention, the next step is a detailed patent search.

Detailed patent searches are best undertaken by specialist searching companies because they have access to patent databases that are not available to non-subscribers. A patent attorney can advise you on this. Find a patent attorney yourself or, preferably, get a recommendation from someone who has gone through the patent filing process themselves. Look for an appropriately qualified attorney or agent. In some countries they will be chartered practitioners.

However, before you approach a patent attorney, as in the case of novelty, undertake a preliminary free patent search yourself using the databases below. Although this search will be limited in its scope it could, at an early stage, reveal prior art that would make your invention not patentable. This would at least save you professional patent search fees—even if it means that you have to start inventing all over again! It is worth pointing out that searches of the public patent databases will only show patent applications that are more than 18 months old—they would not have reached the stage when they are published so that anyone can see what the proposed invention is. Any patent application that is less than 18 months old is not open to public view—that's how the system works.

Patents can be searched on:
- Worldwide Database
  www.epo.org/searching/free/espacenet.html
- US Patent Database
  http://www.uspto.gov/patft/index.html
- Google Patent Search
  https://www.google.com/patents
- Google Advanced Patent Search
  http://www.google.co.uk/advanced_patent_search
- Japanese Patent Database
  http://www.ipdl.inpit.go.jp/homepg_e.ipdl
- PCT Database
  http://patentscope.wipo.int/search/en/search.jsf

To file a patent application

If you have found in your preliminary patent search or your literature search that your invention satisfies the patentability conditions, get a patent attorney to file a patent application on your behalf. Don't be tempted to write your own patent application. However, you can help the patent attorney considerably (and lessen the costs) by providing them with details of the invention as clearly and accurately as possible. It is important to remember that terms and explanations that are familiar to you may need further clarification when describing the invention to the patent attorney.

The patent application will contain details of the following: applicant(s), inventor(s), agent, priority application information, title of invention, description of the invention, claims, drawings, abstract, fee sheet and the filing date. Your main contributions are the clear description of your invention and professional drawings associated with the invention. It is also very important that you give to your patent attorney all priority application information— this is any prior patents or any other information you found during your literature and patent searches that relate to your invention. Your patent attorney will decide what, if any, of this information might be mentioned in your patent application. This may help with the later patent examination process to which your application will be subjected.

The date of filing of the patent application is significant—it is the date that gives your patent application (your invention) a priority date worldwide. This means that any other patent application that is filed at a later date for the same invention as yours will fail because your invention was made earlier and will therefore be given priority over all other such later inventions. Conventional wisdom says that it is important to file a patent application as early as possible, and it is generally right to assume the earlier the better to guarantee a priority claim. However, there may be cases where delaying a filing ought to be considered, for example if there are likely to be significant changes to an invention during its development phase. Much will depend on what you know about your competitors and what they might be doing.

Applying for a patent

Remember, only about 3% of granted patents ever end up as successful commercial products. That can be very discouraging, but you shouldn't let it put you off. When a patent turns into a successful commercial product the rewards—financial and otherwise—can be large.

There are three types of patent application:
1. National patent application.
2. Regional patent application.
3. Patent convention treaty (PCT) application.
   The PCT is an international treaty administered by WIPO, the World Intellectual Property Organisation, based in Geneva. WIPO are the clearing house for international patent applications. At June 2017, the PCT covered 152 countries.

Notice, however, that a patent might start with a national filing, move to PCT and then become a regional filing when the PCT reaches its national phase.
1. National (traditional) patent application
   A national patent application is filed in a particular country at the national patent office. The patent office for each of the WIPO member

states can be found at www.wipo.int. A patent filed in this way is protected and enforced according to the patent laws of the country. A national patent application has to be filed in each country in which patent protection is sought.

This type of patent application is appropriate for an invention which has a market in the country in which the application was filed.

2. Regional patent application

Regional patent applications can be filed at a national or regional patent office. An example of a regional office is the African Regional Intellectual Property Organisation (ARIPO), European Patent Office (EPO) or *l'organisation Africaine de la Propriété intellectuelle*/African Intellectual Property Organisation (OAPI). A single regional patent granted by a regional patent office has effect in all the member states of that region.

3. PCT patent application

PCT—the Patent Cooperation Treaty—is an international treaty which is open to all countries which are a party to the Paris Convention for the Protection of Industrial Property (1883). A PCT is a single filing with one authority. On filing the PCT the applicant effectively buys an option to file in all PCT countries 18 months later. The inventor doesn't have to nominate all of the 152 countries, but many do.

A PCT should be filed—by your patent attorney or patent agent—at a national (or regional) patent office of a member country or at the World Intellectual Property Organisation (WIPO). In the international phase a prior art search is conducted by examiners of the 18 patent offices recognised as PCT International Searching Authorities (ISA). A list of relevant prior art is cited in the international search report (ISR). The examiners also provide an opinion on patentability, that is whether or not the application satisfies the requirements of novelty, inventive step against the prior art, and industrial applicability. The examiners then transmit their search report to WIPO who publish the patent application as well as the search report.

After the international phase the patent enters the national phase in countries where you wish the patent to be granted. It should be understood, therefore, that there is no such thing as 'an international patent' (unlike an international patent application). Each designated country individually grants the patent, charges a national filing fee, and may require a translation of the patent application into a language accepted by the national office.

It is worth noting that renewal fees have to be paid to keep a patent application 'pending' i.e. right up to the time that the patent is granted or rejected. Also, bear in mind that once the patent is granted, fees have to be paid every year for the life of the patent to keep the patent in force. The renewal costs vary from country to country. It is the case that the costs involved in applying for a patent and paying the annual patent fees for the life of the patent in each relevant country are high. This is the reason why the PCT application route is more appropriate for inventions which will lead to products with a global market.

The steps you go through in applying for a patent to the ultimate stage of developing the product are shown in the following flow chart.

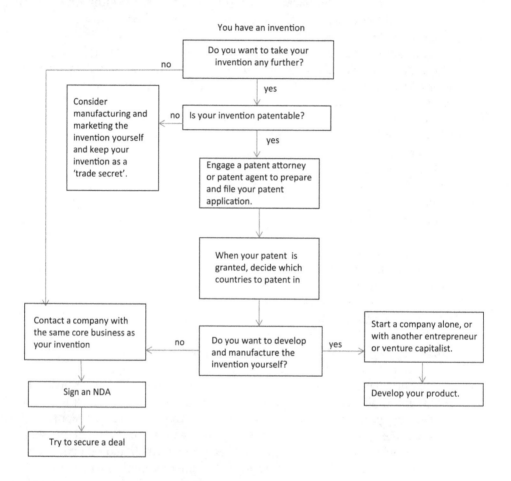

For an overview of the whole PCT system, visit the website of the World Intellectual Property Organization (WIPO): http://www.wipo.int/pct/en/faqs/faqs.html.

The PCT process offers a longer time during which you have opportunities to modify the patent claims after receiving the search report and to decide in which countries you would like to have patent protection.

Other types of intellectual property

Trademarks

Trademarks are distinctive signs that differentiate the goods and services of one provider from those of another. To be registered, a trademark has to be capable of graphic representation and is typically therefore a word, a recognisable image such as a logo, or a combination of these. Specific colours, for instance the red and white Coca-Cola logo, might also be part of a trademark. An audible jingle can be registered as a trademark, as occasionally can a three-dimensional object such as the distinctively shaped Coca-Cola bottle. You register a trademark with national Intellectual Property Offices, as you do a patent. In the UK, for instance, you can register your trademark through the Intellectual Property Office via the government website www.gov.uk/register-a-trademark. Registered marks last for 10 years in the first instance. The ® symbol can be used alongside a mark if it is registered. In some countries the law offers a degree of protection to unregistered marks that are widely recognised and have an established reputation. However, such rights are usually difficult and expensive to enforce compared with a registered trademark which is taken to provide legal proof of an owner's rights in a mark. Generally, a trademark has to be actively used and defended to remain in force.

Copyright

Copyright protects literary and artistic works and applies to journal articles, papers, books, art work, film, television programmes, music, original dramatic and literary work, illustration and photography. It also applies to software code, web content and databases. It means that no-one can, without your permission, copy, reproduce, distribute, perform, broadcast, translate or adapt into other forms, the work you have created.

Copyright is one of the oldest IP rights. The first recorded copyright dispute was a pitched battle between Saint Columba and Saint Finnian in the sixth century. The judgement of the king was: 'To every cow belongs her calf, therefore to every book belongs its copy'. This is still a good if rather pithy definition of copyright. Copyright lasts 75 years after the life of the author and is one of the strongest IP rights—but emphatically doesn't cover ideas, merely the way the idea is expressed. The specific words on the page and the layout of the page itself is covered by a copyright. So, an idea is patentable, an expression is copyrighted.

In most countries copyright is an automatic right. It is good practice to mark your work with the copyright symbol ©, your name and the year it was created, if you wish, but while this indicates that you have the authorship on the work it does not necessarily increase your level of legal copyright protection.

Trade secrets

Strictly speaking, trade secrets are not considered to be intellectual property. Even so, in some countries trade secrets are afforded a degree of protection in law. Trade secrets are know-how or confidential information such as a formula, method, process, the performance characteristics of devices and systems, the chemical composition or ingredients that are particular to a business or product. These will not be generally known to the public but will confer some sort of economic benefit on to the holder and will have had some effort put into keeping them secret. The most famous example of a trade secret is the recipe for Coca-Cola.

Publications to prevent patenting

Some companies deliberately put their un-patented inventions into the public domain, either by publishing them on their website or in professional journals. By doing this they prevent their competitors from obtaining a patent for that technology. This can be a useful ploy if a company has a very large number of inventions and filing a patent for each one would become extremely expensive and may not necessarily generate a financial return.

The main asset in an IDE is often its intellectual property, as we have said, and this is most likely to be its patent portfolio.

Some useful patent-related websites:

http://www.ipo.gov.uk/blogs/equip/

https://www.gov.uk/government/organisations/intellectual-property-office

www.wipo.int/portal/en/

www.wipo.int/patentscope/en/data/developing_countries.html#P11_68

www.uspto.gov

IOP Publishing

Entrepreneurship for Creative Scientists

Dawood Parker, Surya Raghu and Richard Brooks

Chapter 6

Writing a business plan

Everyone will tell you that if you are going to start a company you must write a business plan. Is this really necessary? Absolutely. The exercise of writing any sort of plan for anything at all helps to clarify goals and intentions. A business plan, however, does more than that. It acts as a roadmap for your business, not only clarifying your objectives but showing you how you can plan to achieve those objectives.

A research proposal is based on information which is specific to the areas of expertise of the proposers and therefore is detailed and complete. In contrast, a business plan of an entrepreneur starting a company contains much information which is uncertain and incomplete. As we have seen, an entrepreneur has no alternative but to make decisions on information which is partly incomplete. Writing a business plan can be enormously helpful in that it can enable you—the entrepreneur—to consider various scenarios and can help you to see more clearly what actions might be needed when circumstances change.

What is a business plan?

A business plan is not something you write on the back of an envelope, but it doesn't need to be a 50-page tome either. It does, however, need to contain some very specific information which we will cover step-by-step later in this chapter. Be prepared to be producing about 20 pages of information, and don't worry if you end up with more. You can start with something as uncomplicated as a set of bullet points that focus on the strategy of the company, indicate its milestones, and allow you to work out financial projections. This is the document that will tell you the amount of money needed to get the business off the ground and through its initial phases. It sounds odd that a document that you write will tell *you* anything, but this is what writing a business plan should do. By the time you have answered all the questions that a professional reading a business plan would expect to find answers to, you will know a great deal more about your business than you did before writing your plan.

It is the document you take with you to your bank, to your accountant, and which explains to potential investors what your business is all about. It is the document which allows you to determine how much cash your start-up needs, what stage that cash can get your business to, and what return may be available to a potential investor. It is an important document, the projections in which can—not uncommonly and beneficially—result in a complete re-think of your business strategy. It is the document that can help the founders of a company spot areas of uncertainty in their business. Even in the rare instances where the people starting a company have their own money to put into it to get it going, a business plan is still of great benefit, particularly in finding out when that money is likely to run out.

Why you should write one

Above all else, a business plan can be used to interest, and hopefully convince, potential funders to provide the cash required to get your business started. Your plan will demonstrate to a possible funder that you really understand your product, market, business model and the resources needed to make the business a success. This will show that the key people in the management team (you, for instance) have done their research and know pretty much all there is to know about the business idea.

For hi-tech start-ups there are likely to be many rounds of fund-raising before your product gets to launch. There may be five to 10 rounds of funding before the business is self-sustaining so the business plan will need to include product timescales, be flexible, and show an interested party how you envisage your business developing over several years.

A business plan is not only useful for people outside of the company, you can also use it as an aide memoire as the company progresses. You can use it to remind yourself of why you decided on certain courses of action and to help you to consider the consequences of taking alternative courses of action. A business plan is a one-time snapshot of your business and, as such, is one that has to be taken over and over again. It is an imperfect document which has to be constantly revised through the twists and turns that your company might take. Frequently updating your business plan will help to make sure that your company stays on track.

Before you start

Writing a business plan can be daunting. Before beginning to write your plan, start to gather together the information you will need to include in it. I find it helps to start with the chosen company name followed by two lines that introduce the invention in straightforward terms, for instance 'we have invented a technique for measuring "whatever it might be"'. Then work your way through the following questions, or as many as are relevant, section by section. Don't ignore the ones you can't answer immediately, research them, and take the trouble now to put together data that will help to support your answers. You will have a much clearer picture of what your company is intending to do at the end of this process.

The product and its intellectual property position
- What is the nature of your invention? Describe what it will be able to do.
- What are, or will be, the major applications of the product or service?
- What market need does the product satisfy?
- What is the company's intellectual property position (patent, copyright, trademark, design rights)?
- How comprehensive will the IP protection be?
- How much protection will the IP provide?
- How difficult or how easy is it (or will it be) to reverse engineer the product? How long might it take for some other party to create a similar product?
- Is there any trade secret built in to the company's technology or processes that will act as extra protection?
- What new technologies are in the pipeline that might compete with your product? Are there any factors that would limit their development or acceptance?

Location and legal structure
- What is the best location for the company? This may be influenced by access to regional funding, cost of office space, access to specialised labour, and logistics of product or service supply.
- What is the best legal structure for the company?
- Who will be the initial owners of the company and what proportion of the company will they own?
- Who will be the directors of the company?

The business model
- How is the company going to generate profit from the product or service?
- What are the key revenue streams, cost of sales and operating costs?

The market
- What is the industry sector? Define and describe it.
- How big is this sector now?
- How big will it be in 1 year? 2 years? 3 years? 5 years?
- What are its chief characteristics? What are the major trends in the industry?
- What changes are occurring inside and outside the industry that will affect the business?
- Who are, or will be, the industry's major customers? Specifically, are they major corporates, SMEs or individuals?
- Who will buy the product and why?
- Will demand for the company's product be concentrated among a few big customers or dispersed amongst many customers? What is the route to market?

- What will be the company's market share of each segment it targets for the 1st year? 2nd year? 3rd year?
- Is the company able to address the market directly or will it require partners e.g. distributors, franchisees, licensors?

Competition
- Who is the current competition? What resources are at their disposal?
- Who is the potential competition? What resources are at their disposal?
- How does your business differ from what your competitors offer (or are likely to offer) especially in the eyes of the consumer?
- What is the market share of the competitors?

Product development and regulatory environment
- What is the regulatory environment that governs the product or service e.g. clinical trials, product approvals?
- At what stage of development is the product now?
- What steps are necessary to reach product launch, what approvals are required, how much will it cost and how long will it take?
- Does the company expect to develop the product itself or to partner with others?

People
- What skills and experience will you need to make the company a success?
- How will you attract these individuals to work for the company?

Company location
- What facilities are necessary for operating the company?
- How will the facilities be acquired? Lease? Purchase?
- When will they be acquired?
- What percentage of any proposed financing will go to 'setting up shop'?
- How will these facilities be expanded and at what cost?
- What is the timing of expansion activities?

Manufacturing
- What are the critical supply inputs? How many vendors provide these inputs? What are the lead times for these inputs?
- Is labour readily available? How expensive is the required labour? Are there geographic locations where labour cost is significantly more attractive?
- Will labour have the necessary skills or is training necessary?
- How much of the 'production process' will be subcontracted?
- What is the process by which the service is provided/goods manufactured and supplied (a flow chart is often useful to articulate this).
- What are the standard costs for production at different volume levels and how do overheads, labour costs, the price of materials (if any), and purchased parts effect production costs?

- What are the capital requirements?
- How are the costs for capital investments recovered and over what period of time?
- How does your company set standards for quality and production control?

How to put together your business plan

1. Executive summary

This is the first section. Although it appears at the beginning of the business plan it is sensible to actually write your executive summary after you have completed all the other sections as it is, in fact, a summary of the key highlights of your business plan.

Your executive summary should be written to be compelling and make an immediate impact. State briefly the background to the problem you are addressing, then state how your device addresses the problem and what is unique about it. Your executive summary should include information on the ownership of the business, what the business does, what the size of the market for your product(s) is, how much finance is needed when and for what purpose, and what the exit route of your company will be.

The executive summary is probably the most important section because it may be the only section read by an investor. Or to put that another way, your executive summary needs to make the person reading it want to read the rest of the business plan. The executive summary should be concise and should not dwell on the technical aspects of your invention. Remember the old adage that you never get a second chance to make a first impression. Keep it to only a few paragraphs and certainly not more than two pages. It is important that your summary is realistic but at the same time it needs to give a sense of excitement about your enterprise (it will need to be very exciting to keep someone reading for two pages).

2. The business

The next section should describe in detail what your company does, or proposes to do, and give more details about its products and services. In this section you will describe the vision for the business and why you believe it will be successful.

Topics to cover in this section include:

- History. Even a tiny start-up company has a history. Give details of how the business has come to this point. If the business has evolved out of a research situation, give details of the research (without giving away confidential information) including how it was funded and the reasons for doing the research.
- Current legal structure. Give details of shareholdings if applicable, and how the shareholdings may change.
- Description of the industry your company fits into. Your reader may not be familiar with this industry so avoid using jargon and acronyms.

- Details of the products or services to be provided. Describe the unique selling point (USP) of your product(s). Give details of why the market will buy the product and what are the benefits to the customer of buying your product or service?
- Detail your development plans.
- List all your intellectual property (IP)—trademarks, patents, design rights—and how the IP is being protected.

3. The management team

For a start-up company seeking investment or grant funding, the composition of the management team is crucial. The CVs of each team member should be included in the business plan (usually as appendices) and you should make clear why they are the right people for the job. Innovation-driven enterprises are usually founded around good ideas but it takes an entrepreneur to turn those ideas into a successful business. Often the inventor, and founder of the company, believes himself/herself able to manage the company themselves. Founders often resist advice to delegate the managing directorship of the company to a talented entrepreneur. This is an attitude that will not find favour with investors who generally are of the view that for a company to be successful a crucial component is a good management team.

Topics to cover in this section include:
- Who is in your team.
- Show that they have the requisite skills and experience.
- If you have gaps in your team identify them and explain what skills you still need, why, and what you intend to do about this.

4. The market

In 'the market' section of the business plan, provide an analysis of the market in which the business operates. This shows that there has been thorough research into the business opportunity you are basing your business plan around.

Topics to cover in this section include:
- An industry overview.
- Details about competitors and their pricing policies.
- Details about how the market has developed to date and how it is expected to develop in the future.
- Volumes of sales of competitor products.
- A comparison of competitor products with your own.

5. Marketing plan

Your marketing plan can be included in 'the market' section of the business plan, or you can put it in a separate section.

Topics to cover in this section include:
- Your target market.
- The route to market, for instance direct sales, using agents or distributors.

- Selling costs, for instance how much will a distributor charge you per item sold?
- Exports.

6. Research and development

Even though this document is called a 'business plan' you can still include R&D in it. If further product development is required, state this clearly in the business plan and explain what needs to be done and at what cost. You may find later that you wish to do even more R&D to maintain your market share or to keep your customers happy. Make allowance for this in your business plan.

7. Risks

Every plan has risks and it is important in your business plan to be realistic about these. By describing the risks that the company faces and the actions required to mitigate those risks you show that the Management Team is in control of the company. This gives confidence to anyone reading your business plan.

A SWOT (strengths, weaknesses, opportunities and threats) analysis is often included in the risk section as it is a useful tool to identify risks. We mentioned this in chapter 1, it looks like this:

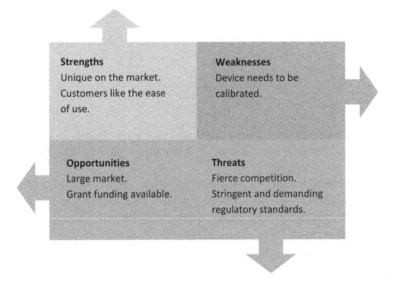

Strengths	**Weaknesses**
Unique on the market. Customers like the ease of use.	Device needs to be calibrated.
Opportunities	**Threats**
Large market. Grant funding available.	Fierce competition. Stringent and demanding regulatory standards.

8. Operations/manufacturing

Assuming that you are going on to manufacture, this is the section in which you explain your vision for manufacture. You will, for instance, outline your reasons for choosing to own or subcontract your manufacturing facilities.

Topics to cover in this section include:
- Details of the manufacturing process you will choose.
- The manufacturing location.

- Details of the premises—type, and owned or subcontracted?
- The facilities required.
- Equipment cost and source.
- Manufacturing costs.
- Cost reduction programmes.

9. **Sensitivity analysis**

It is also useful to show the effect of the major opportunities and threats (SWOT, see above) on your financial projections. Many business plans include a best case and worse case projection as well as the probable one.

10. **Exit**

If you can provide examples of exits of similar businesses then that will help potential investors understand possible future exit routes. These could be trade sales (most likely) or an initial public offering which is the sale of stock by a private company (a floatation on the Stock Exchange) to the public in order to raise capital to expand the business.

In the next chapter we will look in detail at putting a business plan together. When you are researching or discussing your business plan you may find the following definitions useful.

Financial terms—glossary

The main body of a business plan includes a summary of your financial projections and provides the financial detail in the appendices. Here are some of the terms used in business plans.

Sales and revenue

Most companies earn money selling products and services. But sales are only one component of a company's income and do not include all the sources of income in a company.

Revenue, however, represents all the money that the company receives and this might include interest, royalties, fees, donations and others. Sales are useful for determining how efficiently a company returns a profit on its primary business of selling goods and services.

Working capital

For a company to remain solvent it needs working capital to meet its short-term debts when they are due for payment. Working capital is needed mainly for paying staff salaries and settling debts. Working capital is essentially current assets minus current liabilities.

Fixed costs

Fixed costs are those expenses that must be paid regardless of production or sales volume. Common examples are rent, insurance and salaries—it doesn't matter whether your company sells one or thousands of your novel devices, these costs will still have to be paid. They are the fixed costs of the company.

Gross margin

Gross margin is a company's total sales income minus its cost of goods sold (COGS), divided by the total sales income, expressed as a percentage. COGS include those expenses directly associated with the production of the products sold. Overhead costs, taxes, one-time equipment purchases and others are excluded from COGS.

Gross margin is important because it represents the profitability of a company before overhead costs are taken into account, and it is a measure of the success of a product or service.

Cash break-even

The cash break-even is the point in the ongoing operation of the company at which the income from sales of goods equals the fixed and variable costs and cash flow is neither positive nor negative.

Balance sheet

A balance sheet shows the value of a company on a particular date. You can think of it as a snapshot of what the business looked like on that day. The balance sheet gives an overview of the assets and liabilities of your business. It also shows how the business is funded and how the funds are being used.

The balance sheet is an important document because investors generally look at it for insight into how efficiently a company is using its resources and how effectively it can finance itself.

Make your business plan readable!

Write your business plan as though any other person reading it knows nothing about your company. It is, in fact, a very useful exercise to explain your invention to a third-party and ask them what they understood about it, and what they felt was important about it. This will give you an idea of what a potential funder will understand when they read your business plan. You may be surprised to find that what your third-party listener understands about your invention was completely wrong, or what they felt was unique and interesting about it was not something you had particularly focused upon.

Consider that although you may have a great idea and a thorough understanding of the technology, you may not be the best person to communicate these to non-technical people who may be your potential investors. It may be wise to employ someone to re-write your plan to suit the eyes and ears of non-technical investors. A private investor will usually want to quickly assess the risks and potential rewards of investing in your company, and whether your company fits with their interests and other investments.

There was a famous radio broadcaster called Alistair Cook who grew up in the UK but spent most of his adult life in the US. He broadcast a 'Letter from America' each week—for decades to people in the UK, commenting on the current news stories in the US. This broadcast was hugely popular not just for the information he gave, but for its clarity. He explained in an interview that when writing his 'Letter from America' each week he wrote at the top of the page 'Dear Mother'. Know your audience and pitch your business plan to them.

Make sure that your business plan is easy to read, i.e. use a font that is large enough so that the text and figures in a spreadsheet can be easily read. Number your sections, provide an easy to follow index, and make sure that your contact details are obvious. When you show your business plan to anyone make sure that the date on it is no more than a month old.

Offering your business plan to investors

It is prudent to add a disclaimer in a prominent position in your business plan. Make sure that this is done before offering your business plan to potential investors. The disclaimer should say something like:

> This business plan is not a prospectus and does not, and is not intended to, constitute an offer or invitation to invest in securities, nor shall it, or any part of it, be relied upon in any way in connection with an offer to subscribe for shares. Investment in a new business carries high risks as well as the possibility of high rewards. Before investing in a project about which information is given, potential investors are strongly advised to take advice from an authorised person who specialises in advising on this type of investment.

Make sure that there is nothing in your business plan that could be construed as a false claim or could be misleading to a potential investor. If you make statements of fact, make sure you can substantiate them

In some countries, the US and UK for instance, it is an offence for you to offer your business plan to anyone who has not been certified as a potential investor. What this means in the UK is that a private investor interested in your business should show you a certificate that proves they are of 'high net worth' or 'sophistication' as set out in the Financial Services and Markets Act 2000. Check what the law is in your own country.

A private investor is likely to be looking at any number of business plans at a time so you need to make your plan concise and readable. What you are hoping to achieve by giving them your business plan is that they ask to meet you to discuss your company with you.

Chapter 7

A business plan

Let's start by assuming that you've invented, applied for a patent, and developed a novel medical device for detecting an abnormality of the heart called atrial fibrillation. What should a business plan for the device look like? At a later time in the development of the company, when you will require a second and larger round of funding, you will need a more detailed business plan than this one (see appendix). Here is an example of the sort of business plan that might be appropriate to raise initial money for your start-up, be it grants from government or early sources of investment. We've taken an atrial fibrillation monitor, a device we're familiar with, as your invention.

Business plan: Company A

1.0 Executive summary

Chronic atrial fibrillation (AF) is the commonest abnormal heart rhythm seen in medical practice. It causes an increased morbidity and mortality and adds significantly to the burden of healthcare costs. The prevalence of atrial fibrillation increases with age—0.5% of those aged 50–59 years to 8.8% of those aged 80–89—as do the associated risks. There is a three- to six-fold increase of thromboembolic phenomena in those with atrial fibrillation which also accounts for 33% of strokes in elderly people.

Company A has developed a device for detecting AF, a condition that goes largely undetected. The determination can be made within a few seconds and can be used to screen any patient in general practice as well as patients at home who have been diagnosed with AF. The detection of an abnormal heart rhythm associated with AF is achieved at relatively low cost and allows the medical practitioner to refer those patients with suspected AF for ECG examination which will confirm the existence or otherwise of AF.

Company A is seeking first round funding of $700 000 to take the monitor through FDA approval, production and launch in the United States. Company A will pursue specific, definable market segments. We will look to US domestic markets first through agreements with established medical device companies and distributors.

2.0 Business

Company A was founded in 2015 to develop a means of screening patients for AF, and for monitoring those patients who have already been diagnosed with AF. The company was made aware of the need for a simple screening device for AF by Dr X, a practising GP.

Chronic AF is the commonest arrhythmia seen in medical practice. It causes an increased morbidity and mortality and adds significantly to the burden of health care costs. The prevalence of AF increases with age as do the associated risks. It goes largely undetected, as AF can often be an asymptomatic condition. AF is implicated in the aetiology of 33% of strokes in older people. The risk of stroke can be significantly reduced by antiplatelet drugs or anticoagulants, but to benefit from such interventions, individuals with AF need to be identified before an adverse event. Given that AF may be asymptomatic or associated with mild, vague and non-specific symptoms, many individuals remain undiagnosed until an adverse event occurs. Prevention of stroke through screening for AF is highly cost-effective.

Company A has developed and plans to market an AF monitor for use in GP surgeries and in the community, and which can also be used for monitoring diagnosed AF patients in the home. It is a small, portable device that is suitable for use in both medical and non-medical environments.

PROFESSIONAL

PHOTOGRAPH

OF MONITOR

Current legal structure:
   The company is structured as follows:
   Managing Director: NAME
   R&D Director & Senior Engineer: NAME
   Accounts Manager: NAME
   Clinical Trials & Regulatory Affairs Coordinator: To be appointed
   Marketing/Sales Director: NAME
   Consultants: NAMES

Shareholdings:
   NAME: PERCENTAE SHAREHOLDING %
   NAME: PERCENTAGE SHAREHOLDING %
   NAME: PERCENTAE SHAREHOLDING %
   NAME: PERCENTAGE SHAREHOLDING %

Product features

The Company A monitor is easy to operate and quickly shows, via a light indicator, if there is an AF event occurring. The key physical features of the Company A monitor are:

Finger clip sensor
Monitor on/off switch
Monitor display, including green/yellow/red indicator
Pulse rate indicator
Pulse wave form depiction
Benefits to the customer

The Company A monitor provides advantages over other methods of AF detection and monitoring, namely:

- Easy to use
- Small and portable
- Cost-effective
- Rapid event measurement
- Requires no special preparation or removal of clothing
- Suitable for professional and home use
- Suitable for use by both medical professionals and non-medical individuals

Advantages

The Company A monitor can be used to monitor or screen for AF. A medical professional is not required to be present to use the device.

Additional advantages of the Company A monitor over other methods for detecting AF are:

1. It does not require any consumables.
2. It is powered by a rechargeable battery, so an electrical outlet is not used during the process of obtaining readings.
3. The simplicity and ease of use enhance patient compliance and tolerance.
4. It is a reusable device designed for frequent use.
5. A single device can be used for multiple patients (i.e. is not specific to one person).
6. Its readings can be repeated immediately (i.e. no re-initiation required).
7. It uses colour coding to indicate relative degree of variation from normal sinus rhythm (e.g. green = good patient condition, red = indication to follow up with further testing by a medical professional).
8. It is non-invasive, comfortable, generally familiar, and extremely easy to use.
9. It gives a very quick indication of the presence of an AF episode (beneficial particularly in emergency situations).
10. It can help to alleviate stress in AF patients by giving them the mechanism to do quick checks for themselves.

11. It has low manufacturing and use costs.
12. It has the potential to minimize the required number of routine cardiac-related physician visits by AF patients.

Details of intellectual property
US patent application NUMBER was filed in DATE.
European Patent Application NUMBER was filed in DATE.

The Company A monitor uses light to detect the pulse at the tip of the finger via a finger-clip sensor. The patient places their finger in the clip which contains an LED and a detector. Visible light then shines through the finger and the detector collects a waveform that represents the heartbeat. The monitor compares the patient's waveform with a template and judges the variance from a regular rhythm.

3.0 The management team

CVs are attached in the appendices to this business plan.

Managing Director, NAME, is a successful entrepreneur and is associated with the development and launch of products PRODUCT NAME, PRODUCT NAME and PRODUCT NAME, having been Managing Director of COMPANY NAME from 1994 to 1999, and COMPANY NAME from 2000 to 2015 and took these companies from start-up to highly successful businesses. He has a PhD in medical instrumentation. NAME is responsible for the business activities of the company including fund-raising.

R&D Director, NAME, is the founder of Company A and is responsible for leading the technical team. NAME has a PhD in patient monitoring techniques and extensive research and business experience. NAME spent the past 2 years as technical manager at COMPANY NAME, a leading medical devices company.

Accounts Manager, NAME, is the Accounts Manager for Company A and works closely with the Managing Director to determine the financial strategies of the company and creates the company budgets. Later, the accounts manager will work closely with a Sales Director (to be appointed) to determine how to maximise the company's profits.

Marketing Manager, NAME, is responsible for the marketing strategy of Company A. NAME has a degree in SUBJECT from UNIVERSITY and has close relations with distributors in Europe and the Far East. NAME will be helping the company to sell its products in these countries among others. The position currently is part-time. NAME also has experience in the manufacturing and regulatory requirements of medical devices.

Consultants
NAME is a consultant to Company A. NAME is a Professor of Medicine at UNIVERSITY and has many years' experience in consulting for major international medical and pharmaceutical companies.

NAME has more recently become a consultant to the company. NAME is a Cardiologist and highly regarded expert in atrial fibrillation. NAME has extensive publications in this area.

4.0 The market

4.1 *Estimated market size*

A market survey carried out by NAME OF MARKET SURVEY COMPANY for Company A indicated that the AF screening device has applications in two main areas. These are:

▼ Home monitoring of AF or at-risk patients
▼ Quick screening of patients for AF in environments such as:
    ▼ Medical professional
        – Physician's offices
        – Ambulances
        – Emergency rooms
    ▼ Non-medical
        – Sporting events
        – Commercial and industrial spaces
        – Schools
        – Other recreational/community facilities

This survey researched the current sales of all products of this type currently available commercially in the US and Europe/Japan. The sales for home, medical and non-medical use are shown below.

Market segment	Total	Basis
Home use	$1.75	Number of AF patients
Medical professional use—PCO/emergency medical equipment	$0.68B	Number of medical stationary and ambulatory medical facilities
Non-medical professional (as emergency medical equipment)	$6.73B	Number of academic, industrial and recreational facilities

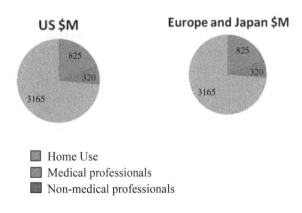

US $M   Europe and Japan $M

■ Home Use
■ Medical professionals
■ Non-medical professionals

Figures based on US market information and extrapolated to the European and Japanese markets, with an assumed monitor selling price of $375.

Strong market interest has been obtained both in the US and the UK through demonstration of prototypes. Company A exhibited the monitor at NAME OF CONGRESS in the US as well as NAME OF CONFERENCE in the UK. In both instances, strong support for the monitor was received from cardiologists and electrophysiologists from around the world.

A major market for the monitor will be in home monitoring. Patients already diagnosed with AF, who are at risk of AF, or who have recently undergone surgery for the condition will be able to self-monitor in the home environment.

World medical device market and trends

As people in the US and Europe age, the inherent demand for healthcare will continue to grow. In the US alone, about 13 000 individuals are expected to turn 60 each day over the next 20 years. Since most healthcare in the US is linked to Medicare the funding for healthcare is expected to be stable. Increasing expenditure on healthcare by governments around the world is driving the global demand for medical devices.

Healthcare reform in the US as well as in other parts of the world has resulted in greater focus on preventative care products and treatments as well as earlier detection of chronic diseases. These trends are positive for market entry and acceptance of the Company A monitor. The US is the largest consumer of medical instruments, equipment and supplies. The country's market was valued at nearly $80 billion in 2005.

The competition within the medical device industry, however, has risen as an increasing number of multinational companies are trying to make their mark in the global market. As a consequence, international sales, joint ventures, mergers and acquisitions are commonplace. Medical device companies are looking at developing economies as an opportunity to drive future growth.

According to 'Global Cardiac Medical Devices—An Analytical Report, 2009–2015', published in February 2011, the global Cardiac Medical Devices market is forecast to reach US$65.6 billion by 2015 at a CAGR of 9.8% during the analysis period 2009–2015. The North American segment accounts for approximately 40% of the global value. Europe claims nearly 30% of the market. Asia-Pacific is the fastest-growing region with a CAGR of 11.6%, driving a market value of US$17.9 billion by 2015.

The 'cardiac rhythm management' market segment, which would include the Company A monitor, accounts for nearly 35% of the overall market. The following table describes the respective market value (2015) and CAGR (2009–2015) as per Axis Research Mind forecasts.

Segment	Expected market value by 2015—(US$ Billion)	CAGR-% forecasts (2009–2015)
Cardiac rhythm management devices (CRM)	22.3	9.3
Interventional cardiac devices (ICD)	15.7	9.9
Cardiac monitoring and diagnostic devices (CM&D)	12.3	11.0
Peripheral vascular devices (PVD)	5.5	9.7
Electrophysiology (EP) devices	4.4	9.7
Cardiac prosthetic devices (CPD)	2.9	9.5

Details about competitors and their pricing policies

An ECG is sometimes performed as part of a full physical examination by a physician to detect the presence of abnormalities in the heart functionality. An ECG is a non-invasive recording of the rhythm of the heart. It requires that the patient spend some time being prepared for and undergoing the test, and it requires the removal of clothing and therefore a private, closed space for the test to be done. There are two parts to the cost associated with an ECG—having the test performed by a medical professional and having the ECG analysed. In the US Medicare reimbursement for the test is $64, but the amount charged and billed varies widely.

COMPETITOR A...
COMPETITOR B...
COMPETITOR C...
COMPETITOR D...

Low-cost ECG monitors do not compete with the Company A monitor. Many ECG-based monitors require a technician or nurse to administer. All require a doctor to interpret the result. As a screening measure this is an expensive process. The Company A monitor allows for multi-location testing which is quick and relatively unsupervised. The monitor gives the result and according to our research only 8% of those requiring an ECG will not have AF. In the home the monitor is very simple to use.

Customer base

The initial target customer base for the Company A monitor is home monitoring of AF for at-risk patients. The doctor and the patient have much to gain in terms of optimised treatment plans through the use of the Company A monitor for home patient monitoring. It is anticipated that the customer base will be quite dispersed, with several patients sharing a common prescribing physician or medical group.

The second market focus will be the quick screening of patients for AF by medical professionals in environments such as physician's offices and emergency care facilities. In such applications, the customer will be the medical care facilities. The incentive for adoption is the ability to quickly screen patients for AF as part of routine vital sign checks. Each care facility is likely to require multiple units. The market will be dispersed, although as a priority in market approach, affiliated care facilities (groups) will be targeted.

The third target customer base for the Company A monitor is its use as emergency medical equipment by non-medical professionals in environments such as recreational facilities, community facilities, schools and commercial locations. In such applications, the Company A monitor will be used for on-site episodes where cardiac distress is suspected. The information gathered by the monitor can be quickly and easily obtained and communicated to emergency medical personnel prior to or upon arrival at the scene. Again, the market will be dispersed. Areas of adoption are suspected to be concentrated geographically as well as by type of facility.

5.0 Marketing plan

Company A intends to introduce the monitor into the medical practice and home AF monitoring market segment in the US. Approving and initiating such uses will be the medical practitioner (cardiologist, electrophysiologist, etc). In order for this to happen the medical community will be made aware of the benefits of the device. We intend to reach this professional group through an already-established sales and distribution channel for products in this same arena. We will explore options for business arrangements that will allow for this to happen. The same is true for product support and service. Discussions are underway to achieve this. Once the initial market entry is solidly established in the US, marketing and sales efforts will be expanded to Europe and beyond in this same segment.

The non-medical community for AF screening will be addressed subsequently to the medical and home-care market segments. The non-medical community is likely to be a highly-segmented market space (businesses, sporting arenas, community centres, etc). Successful entry into this market will be highly dependent upon regulatory requirements regarding the benefits of AF screening on site at non-medical facilities and functions.

The steps in this marketing plan are shown in the following flow-chart:

Initial marketing
Paperwork and contracts in place
Complete assembly and packaging
Number of units, turnaround time,
cost and 'ship to' determined

Act on sales and marketing strategy
Identify and evaluate partner options
Select partner(s)
Establish contractual agreements

Product support
Who, how, where,
costs determined

Expand market presence
Penetrate secondary and
tertiary market spaces

Establish strategy for sales & marketing
Consider:
Partnering with large company
Partnering with distributor
Various business models, e.g. lease vs sell
Understand the sales cycle

Storage/warehousing
Location and
responsibility determined

Begin commercial sales
Initial target market
Selling or lease price set
Product Warranty

6.0 Research and development

The documentation for the Company A monitor is currently being prepared for compliance testing and for FDA approval. Company A has engaged regulatory experts who are advancing the application process. We expect to have achieved these objectives by the end of the year.

The company is awaiting a revised quotation for the production of the first 500 monitors from NAME OF MANUFACTURING COMPANY.

Company A is seeking to establish its product in the marketplace through outsourced manufacturing and distribution agreements. Associated objectives include:

1. Complete the in-progress regulatory (FDA and CE) application processes with the help of contracted regulatory experts.
2. Obtain regulatory clearances.
3. Obtain financing to pursue initial manufacture and market introduction.
4. Establish agreement(s) with strategically selected distributors.
5. Initiate product manufacture for market introduction.
6. Build staff and infrastructure to support ongoing manufacturing oversight and technical support.
7. Continue R&D and product development.

Fully-functional prototypes have been manufactured and are being used for product demonstration purposes as well as required device testing purposes.

All device testing and documentation required for regulatory applications are near completion. The application for FDA clearance of the Company A monitor as a medical device is planned for submission next year. Full-scale manufacturing will commence immediately following receipt of the clearance along with initial marketing efforts.

7.0 Barriers and risks

Market entry of the Company A monitor assumes regulatory (FDA) clearance is received. Clinical studies have been conducted in the US and UK, both of which have produced data that clearly support the technical efficacy of the device. Use of the screening and monitoring device is aligned with current overall cost-lowering and preventative healthcare trends.

In order for the home monitoring of AF patients using the Company A monitor to be widely adopted, medical professionals must be aware of the device and its capabilities. In the US a physician's prescription will be required for patient use. The low cost of the device and simplicity of use will be largely advantageous in patient use applications.

Use of the Company A monitor by medical professionals for the screening of patients for AF on a routine basis will be dependent upon awareness of the device and its capabilities and benefits. Company A plans to address this by launching industry awareness campaigns along with physician training and materials.

Use of the Company A monitor as emergency medical screening/monitoring equipment by non-medical professionals in community, work, and recreational facilities, will be dependent upon aligning with personal safety trends in such facilities. It will also be dependent on obtaining validation from medical professionals, including emergency medical professionals, that such on-site AF screening is warranted and beneficial.

Target markets for Company A monitor

Market	Technical hurdles	Regulatory hurdles	Buyer focus	Market size
Home monitoring of AF patients	LOW	LOW	HIGH	$1.1B
Medical professional use—PCP/emergency medical equipment	LOW	LOW	HIGH	$0.43B
Non-professional emergency medical equipment	LOW	LOW	MEDIUM	$4.2B

8.0 Operations/manufacturing

The company will establish its product in the marketplace though outsourced manufacturing and distribution agreements. A company to do the initial, full-scale manufacturing of the devices has been identified. Pricing, quantities, lead times and other terms are under discussion. The company is also in discussion with selected distributors. The company is planning to build staff to provide technical support to ongoing manufacture.

9.0 Sensitivity analysis

If you have chosen to include a SWOT analysis in the risks section, here is your opportunity to outline what the SWOT analysis could lead to.)

10.0 Exit

The company's preferred exit route is a trade sale. Businesses similar to Company A have achieved significant trade sales in recent years. We expect that we could be a candidate for a trade sale within 5 years.

Finance

When you start a company you usually have some idea of when you expect to begin to make a profit and what your profits might be over a 5 year period after that. But what you really need to know with more than a hunch is how much money you will need during the period between start-up and making a profit. You will also need to know whether you will need the money all at once at start-up, and if there are times later on when you will need further injections of cash. These may be difficult to work out but you will have to derive these from your business plan.

Let's assume that your start-up needs to raise $700 000 for a percentage stake in the company. The investment will be used to manufacture the first 2000 devices and will take the company to the beginning of year 1 sales. The table shows how the $700 000 will be spent.

Itemised cost categories	Cost up to the milestone of manufacturing first 2000 units
CEO	$125 000
Sales and marketing	$50 000
Education and advertising	$10 000
Accounting	$12 000
Legal	$9000
Marketing	$8000
Trade shows	$18 000
Office support	$15 000
Miscellaneous	$20 000
R&D and technical support	$25 000
Facilities	$8000
Manufacturing	$400 000
Total	**$700 000**

Let's also assume that the cost of manufacturing a device, the variable cost per unit is $285.00, as shown below and that you will sell the devices at $375.00, giving a gross margin of $90.00.

Manufacturing	$200.00
Distribution	$60.00
Warehousing	$10.00
Shipping	$15.00
Variable costs/unit	**$285.00**
Pricing and contribution	
Unit price	$375.00
Margin	$90.00

Let's assume also that, just for example, the fixed costs are $590 000 for the first 2 years and will increase in subsequent years. Fixed costs are made up of payroll, regulatory costs, facilities, office expenses, advertising, accounting, legal costs and marketing.

The cash flow projection and market penetration are shown in table 7.1.

Table 7.1. Cash flow projection with market penetration.

Sales	$671 633	$3 821 250	$11 107 500	$35 047 500	$69 074 100
Number of units	1791	10 190	29 620	93 460	184 198
Selling Price/unit	£375	£375	£375	£375	£375
Fixed costs	$590 000	$590 000	$600 000	$1 200 000	$2 400 000
Variable costs/unit	$285	$245	£220	$220	$220
Total variable costs	$510 441	$2 496 550	$6 516 400	$20 561 200	$40 523 472
Total outgoings	$1 100 441	$3 086 550	$7 116 400	$21 761 200	$42 923 472
Cash flow	**$428 808**	**$734 700**	**$3 991 100**	**$13 286 300**	**$26 150 628**

The cash flow is detailed in the following spreadsheets. Firstly, the figures for year 1 to year 5 are shown indicating a very impressive profit from year 3 (remember—this is only an example!). Secondly, over the first 2 years the cash flow is broken down into months. In this example, breakeven occurs at month 23, quite a good prospect for the company. These figures also indicate that at this rate of growth the company will not need further cash within the first 5 years.

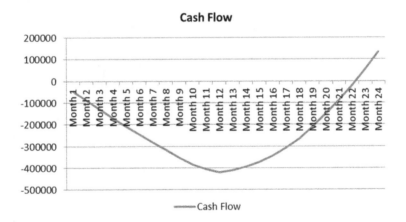

An initial business plan like this, for example, is what you would include in an application for grant funding or even present to angel investors who would be interested in getting involved in your start-up at an early stage.

	Month 1	Month 2	Month 3	Month 4	Month 5	Month 6	Month 7	Month 8	Month 9	Month 10	Month 11	Month 12
Unit Price	375	375	375	375	375	375	375	375	375	375	375	375
Sales	1	90	100	100	100	150	150	150	150	200	300	400
Rolling sales	1	91	191	291	391	541	691	841	991	1191	1491	1891
Fixed Costs	49100	49100	49100	49100	49200	49200	49200	49200	49200	49200	49200	49200
Variable cost per unit	285	285	285	285	285	285	285	285	285	285	285	285
Total variable costs	285	25650	28500	28500	28500	42750	42750	42750	42750	57000	85500	114000
Income	375	33750	37500	37500	37500	56250	56250	56250	56250	75000	112500	150000
Outgoings	49385	74750	77600	77600	77700	91950	91950	91950	91950	106200	134700	163200
Income minus outgoings	-49010	-41000	-40100	-40100	-40200	-35700	-35700	-35700	-35700	-31200	-22200	-13200
Cash flow	-49010	-90010	-130110	-170210	-210410	-246110	-281810	-317510	-353210	-384410	-406610	-419810

	Month 13	Month 14	Month 15	Month 16	Month 17	Month 18	Month 19	Month 20	Month 21	Month 22	Month 23	Month 24
Unit Price	375	375	375	375	375	375	375	375	375	375	375	375
Sales	450	500	550	600	650	700	800	850	850	900	950	1000
Rolling sales	2341.00	2841.00	3391.00	3991.00	4641.00	5341.00	6141.00	6991.00	7841.00	8741.00	9691.00	10691.00
Fixed Costs	49100	49100	49100	49100	49200	49200	49200	49200	49200	49200	49200	49200
Variable cost per unit	245	245	245	245	245	245	245	245	245	245	245	245
Total variable costs	110250	122500	134750	147000	159250	171500	196000	208250	208250	220500	232750	245000
Income	168750	187500	206250	225000	243750	262500	300000	318750	318750	337500	356250	375000
Outgoings	159350	171600	183850	196100	208450	220700	245200	257450	257450	269700	281950	294200
Income minus outgoings	9400	15900	22400	28900	35300	41800	54800	61300	61300	67800	74300	80800
Cash flow	9400	25300	47700	76600	111900	153700	208500	269800	331100	398900	473200	554000

Chapter 8

Raising funds

Having armed yourself with a business plan, your next crucial task is to start the process of raising the funding that your company will need to take it through the early stages of its development. This can be a harrowing experience, probably the most stressful part of starting a company. The reason for this is that start-up companies with technology at an early stage of development are viewed as high-risk by investors and are generally avoided. US investors are considered to be more favourably disposed towards high tech start-ups than anywhere else. In the UK, recent changes in tax legislation have made UK investors less risk-averse than they have been reputed to be.

However, much of the reluctance to invest in start-up companies is not unexpected. Many start-ups fail and the number that survive and prosper are small as we've discussed earlier with the 'valley of death' illustration. It is often said that for every ten high-tech companies started only one will survive and be successful.

But that is no reason to give up. Let's continue our quest for money. You might think of seeking a loan from a bank for your start-up. This is unlikely to be successful unless the loan can be secured against your personal assets. You may not be willing, or be in a position, to provide such security so we may well have to conclude that an approach to a bank is a non-starter.

Another source of finance is through contacts, often referred to as 'the three Fs'— friends, family and fools. If seeking finance through this route be sure to emphasize the risks involved in their investment and do whatever you can to avoid allowing people to invest for purely sentimental reasons. Also consider whether even borrowing from friends and family is best for your long-term happiness. People can often interpret what you describe as 'risk' as you merely understating your abilities.

An option

Scientists are often involved in leading-edge fundamental research. It is possible that this may attract the attention of a larger company. This can lead to the larger company partly or fully funding your company to undertake further research in this specialised area in exchange for exclusive access to the research—taking 'an option'. By this I mean that they will fund your research and have access to it for, say, 12 or 18 months, during which time you agree that you will not approach any other company to try to interest them commercially in your technology. At the end of this exclusive option period the large company has the option, i.e. the exclusive right, to negotiate with you for further access to your technology, for instance to obtain a licence or purchase it. You, in turn, have to agree to negotiate reasonably—you cannot negotiate unreasonably hoping that the negotiations will fail because you have another company in mind that might want to buy your technology for more money! The advantage of this exclusive option approach is that you have the benefit of the funding and have given up no equity during the exclusive access period. In this way, the start-up benefits from funding for its research and consequently may also secure a licensing agreement or even equity investment in the company. Any of these would be a significant achievement in the early life of a start-up. It should be recognised though that such arrangements are not common as a means of raising funds for a start-up.

The grant route

Because many investors regard high-tech start-ups as too risky it is not surprising that start-ups commonly start their fund-raising by seeking grants from government or regional or local authorities. The attraction of grant funding is that grants are generally non-repayable and can be up to 100% of total project costs. A particular advantage of some of these grants to start-ups is that they are available for research and development long before even proof-of-principle has been demonstrated. Government is almost always the sole source of funding for fundamental research and development.

Be aware that grant funding may come with conditions. Some grants will require the researcher to publish the information derived under the grant. Some may even restrict the derived information from being sold to a commercial company on an exclusive basis. A company in Europe, for example, that has received a government grant may in some cases find that it is not possible to assign the derived information to any commercial company outside the EU for several years, except with permission from the granting authority. Nevertheless, grant funding can be an excellent way of taking your invention on just one stage further towards proof of principle.

In the UK, for example, there are many government grants available for start-ups. These grants cover a range of awards from cash awards to buying equipment or assistance in acquiring premises. Most small business grants are awarded to help launch a start-up with the aim to generate jobs and stimulate the economy.

A good starting point for a start-up seeking grants in the UK is the Business Finance Support Finder on the gov.uk website: https://www.gov.uk/business-finance-support. The Welsh Government also lists grants available to start-ups at its Business Grants website: http://gov.wales/funding/grants/business/, and in

Scotland the Scottish Government has a similar list: https://www.mygov.scot/funding-advice-search/.

Most commonly, a direct grant is money given to a start-up to cover investment in equipment, training or opening up new markets. Most grants will be for around 60% to 70% of the total funds required so that the start-up has to make a contribution. Funds up to £0.5m can be available.

Look particularly at the Innovate UK website: www.gov.uk/government/organisations/innovate-uk. Innovate UK is the UK's innovation agency. The agency supports companies, including start-ups, to drive the science and technology innovations that will grow the UK economy. Innovate UK collaborates with companies in many sectors of science and technology and in most cases could be the first port of call for a start-up seeking grant funding.

In many countries around the world there are funds available for R&D, innovation, employment, training, etc. Finding the sources can be time-consuming and in any case these incentives constantly change as their effectiveness is evaluated by government. Nevertheless, finding the most appropriate source of funding for your start-up whether it is in your own locality, region, country or elsewhere, is certainly worth the effort because of its undoubted benefits to your company. In this regard the 'Survey of Global Investment and Innovation Incentives' https://www2.deloitte.com/global/en/pages/tax/articles/global-investment-and-innovation-incentives-survey.html is a valuable source of information giving the government incentives that are available in 36 countries for R&D, employment, training, etc.

For those scientists familiar with writing research grant applications, seeking funding for a start-up or from government can be quite a different task. In an application or presentation for funds you, as the scientist and entrepreneur, will be required to present information often outside your area of expertise, the sort of information expected in a business plan. This is where it is so important to have the backing of a dedicated management team of different skills who can contribute to such an application covering not only the technology but also all the other business aspects such as customers, pricing, market surveys, risks, financial projections, etc.

Incentives for UK investors

UK government legislation in recent years has acted as an incentive for investors to invest in UK companies including start-ups. The Seed Enterprise Investment Scheme (SEIS) is a tax relief scheme which allows investors to offset eligible investment against their tax bill, thus significantly reducing their capital risk. The relief allows investors to claim back up to 78% of their investment through tax. As a result, many investors now require a start-up to be approved for SEIS before they will consider investing in it. To obtain SEIS status, a start-up needs to apply to HMRC and get approval. Currently the SEIS scheme is not open to employees of the company, but it is open to company Directors if they have less than a 30% stake in the company. The rules regarding applying for and making use of the SEIS scheme are laid out in: https://www.gov.uk/guidance/venture-capital-schemes-apply-to-use-the-seed-enterprise-investment-scheme.

The second major tax relief investment scheme, the Enterprise Investment Scheme (EIS) is for companies at a later stage. Approved start-ups can get their investors back a significant part of their investment in tax benefits. Investors can claim up to 30% back in tax on investments and can also defer capital gains tax on such shares. See: https://www.gov.uk/guidance/venture-capital-schemes-apply-for-the-enterprise-investment-scheme.

So, while SEIS and EIS are not grant funding, they certainly significantly reduce the risk of investing in a start-up. Getting approval for your start-up from HMRC for SEIS and/or EIS should help you raise funds for your start-up.

Crowdfunding

Crowdfunding is another way of raising money, usually from a large number of people and most commonly via the internet. Crowdfunding consists of the project initiation, the people who support the project, and the moderating organisation—the 'platform'—that coordinates the parties.

Some crowdfunding platforms are specifically aimed at scientific research, such as experiment.com, petridish.com, consano.org and flatphysica.com. Others are more general such as ourcrowd.com and kickstarter.com.

There are two types of crowdfunding, equity crowdfunding and rewards crowdfunding. depending on the level of funding given, the rewards to the giver can vary from 'our heartfelt thanks' to prototypes and fully working products. The 3D virtual reality hardware Oculus Rift was originally funded through Kickstarter. Kickstarter backers pledged a certain amount in order to receive a first-generation developer's kit. When Oculus was bought by Facebook and a commercial model of the Rift was released, the Kickstarter backers who had received the original development kit then also received a free consumer version.

Crowdfunding is likely to be particularly useful for initial developmental research, but the money asked for and raised is usually fairly low. But whatever fund-raising route you decide to take, you will have to make presentations to potential investors.

Pitching for funds

Your first exposure to potential funders of your business is usually a 'pitch' that you make to them to get their interest in your company. Investors generally do not want to hear about the detail of your technology, especially at the first meeting with them. They will, however, be curious about the solution to a problem that your invention is offering and they would certainly want to see and listen to you if you are an individual who will inspire others to feel excited about your invention.

If you choose to give potential investors written materials then it might be worthwhile taking a look at *Impact* by Jon Moon [1]. This is a book on how to make written communications succinct whilst containing a wow-factor, that is how to make yours compete successfully with everything else that is out there.

Early as it may seem, pictures of your invention/product and a video are hugely impactful. You need a website, and social media accounts where potential investors can register their interest.

In your pitch to your investors you will present a 'pitch-deck' which is usually a set of approximately 10 slides which supports a presentation of around 10 minutes and is generally followed by 10 minutes of questions. Make sure you say who you are, why people need your product or service, what your company does, emphasise your achievements to date and make very clear what it is that you want. Your objective with your pitch-deck is to hear the magic words: 'That sounds interesting, I would like to know more, let's arrange a meeting.' The importance of your set of slides cannot be overestimated. A recent study suggests that investors spend less than 4 min on average looking at them so you've got very little time to make an impression!

Whenever possible, show your potential investors a demonstrator, i.e. a mock-up of the concept of the product you are proposing to develop. It often greatly clarifies what you are presenting. There is no harm in showing an attractive, compelling demonstrator, no matter how 'optimistic' it might be.

It can happen that your pitch may not be what you finally obtain funding for. As an example, Dr Amir Shadmand and Dr Anouseh Tavakoli worked on a collaborative research project with Greenwich University, UK, using Near Field Communication (NFC) technology and a data mining algorithm for tourist applications. This led to the development of NFC energy harvesting technology which in turn led to an enhanced Smartphone case with built-in game controller (see www.flitchio.com)—not what they originally had in mind.

Pitching to investors

Before approaching anyone for investment in your company, bear in mind that start-up high-tech companies are very high risk. Many start-ups fail as we've discussed before. Even though in some countries there are schemes that can minimise losses in start-ups, it is quite possible to lose money investing in a start-up. Further, make investors aware that investing in a start-up is unlikely to provide them with a return on their investment for a few years, if at all. It would be prudent to encourage them to undertake research about the start-up and in any case to consult their financial advisor before deciding on an investment.

The topics you'll cover in your pitch are close to the ones in your business plan but how you present these should be very, very different! Yes, investors will want to know about your company, your management team, what problem your invention solves, your target market, the competition you're likely to encounter and your business strategy. But how you present this information in a pitch is crucial if you hope to get investors interested.

Perfect pitch

As we've said, pitching for funds from investors can be a frightening experience and particularly if you have only a few minutes to excite your audience to part with their money. But what will help is to bear the following in mind:

- Investors are less interested in your idea or the technology than they are in your strategy for its execution. It's commonly said that a brilliant idea with poor execution is worthless. Tell them about your business experience and track record and project an image of someone who is the driving force behind the technology. Indicate why your technical solution is unique, who your customers are and what revenues it will deliver and when. Be frank about the risks your start-up is likely to encounter and what you will do to overcome or minimise those risks.
- Make only realistic claims when addressing investors for funds. Getting investors excited with exaggerated claims may be tempting, but remember these will inevitably be subjected to a subsequent due diligence process by interested investors and you will be found out!
- Speak clearly and at a pace that will enable your audience to take in everything you have to say. Avoid jargon and speak to make an impact on the investors. Spend much less time describing your technology. Make your pitch an informative and enjoyable experience for your audience. A smiley face helps, a stern one doesn't—they wouldn't want to work with a humourless entrepreneur for the next few years.
- Try to get audience participation sometime during or after your presentation. Who knows, someone may have seen a great opportunity for your technology, much more than you had in mind to start with. This is what you want—audience participation.

Your pitch-deck

When pitching to investors you usually do this by presenting your case in about 10 slides showing the following:

SLIDE 1
A brief profile of your company, the business you are in and the stage the business is at. Tell them about your management team, your IP position and why your product has an advantage over competitors. Say clearly what you're asking for and what share of the company you're prepared to give the investors

SLIDE 2
Give the details of all the members of your management team including the future appointments you intend to make.

SLIDE 3
Give a very brief description of your novel product emphasizing the problem it solves. Clearly state how it would benefit the customer and why it is better than the competition.

SLIDE 4

Give the details you have about your target market and the business opportunity that this presents. State also the potential for growth in this business sector and your strategy for addressing your target market segments.

SLIDE 5

Be open about the competition but stress the advantages of your product.

SLIDE 6

Illustrate clearly to your potential investors how you intend to make money and generate profits and the time-scale for doing this. Some of the financial statements in your business plan could be included here.

SLIDE 7

Clearly state your route to market, your milestones and timescale.

SLIDE 8

State the risks to your business as you see them and explain how you propose to overcome or minimize these. Outline your contingency plans to cope with serious risks.

SLIDE 9

End by repeating what you are asking for and state, in a compelling way, that your business offers investors a great opportunity.

SLIDE 10

Invite the audience to participate in your presentation by encouraging questions and comments.

Try to avoid slides that are just lots of words or bullet points. Use striking images, in particular good images of your product or what you envisage your product will look like. Your audience are more likely to remember facts and figures if you visually present them, or if you explain them in an engaging way, rather than listing them on a dull slide. Aim for your presentation to be no more than 10 minutes.

Build a rapport with the audience and, as the entrepreneur, show excitement for the project and your commitment to it. You should elaborate on your relevant expertise in the project and explain your role in the business. Present yourself and your team with confidence. Remember, it is generally accepted that investors are most commonly influenced by management, management and management! Name your management team with their position in the company and their professional background and experience. Don't hesitate to mention gaps in your team and what you intend to do about these.

It is vital that you say clearly what problem your invention will solve. Demonstrate an early prototype or show an image of the proposed product. Emphasise its benefits but avoid dwelling on its details and specifications. It is important to stress what is unique about the product which gives it the advantage over all other similar products. Give details about the market research you've done indicating the market size in customer numbers and sales, the projected growth over at least five years and your strategy for reaching your target markets. Indicate also the effect, if any, on your business model of competition in future years. Mention any products that may be considered competitive, the investors would certainly find out about those anyway.

Investors want to know how your company will make money. Summarise what's in your business plan about your future revenues and how the business can be scaled up. The growth in your business is of great importance to investors who, always bear in mind, will invest in your high-risk start-up only if they can see a significant multiple return on their investment, an expectation of 20–40 times is quite usual.

Indicate clearly the route to market for your product, including the marketing and sales channels you propose to use. Be honest about the risks that you have identified in the development of your product and indicate how you intend to minimise or eliminate these risks. Again, the risk factors and your ability to cope with them may well be what ultimately determines whether you get investment or not.

Throughout the pitch make very clear what you are asking for and why investing in your start-up offers them a great opportunity. Most often in a start-up you'll be looking for an amount of money for a negotiable equity stake in your company. If this is so, say so, and be as convincing as you can. The investors would want to see someone who is credible and passionate about the project and who will remain committed to the company whatever the hurdles that have to be overcome. Commitment to the company is a very important requirement for investors. This should be a warning to innovators who believe that a part-time commitment to their start-up will be adequate—not uncommon among inventors who wish to retain their tenured, full-time posts. Investors are unlikely to be satisfied that their funds are in safe-hands if you only have a part-time commitment to your company. The suspicion is that when the going gets tough you will withdraw into the safety of a full-time job and neglect your commitment to the company.

As we've said earlier, raising finance for your business is most often a stressful experience. Further, the process is also likely to take much longer than you might expect and that is even after an investor has agreed to invest. Nevertheless, money has to be raised so let's see what might be available to a start-up. At least with what you now know about pitching for investment you should be in a better position to make creditable presentations to investors. After grant funding let's see what other type of finance may be available for your start-up.

If your start-up is at the stage where it has exhausted its R&D grant funding but still needs finance for further research and before proof of principle has been shown, then what you'll be looking for is seed funding usually for sums up to about £50 000. It may be possible to attract private investors, 'business angels', at this stage of your business. These are high net worth individuals who typically invest between £10 000 and £25 000 in such start-ups. It helps if you are putting in money yourself. These business angels usually have many different reasons for investing and they can often bring not only money but also business experience to the start-up. In the UK, business angels can now benefit from tax relief under the Seed Enterprise Investment Scheme (SEIS) and the Enterprise Investment Scheme (EIS) which might make investment in your start-up perhaps a little more attractive to them.

If you're a start-up that's gone beyond proof-of-principle and have a working prototype you're probably looking for finance in the range up to £500 000. Some of this could well be available as government grants but the rest would most likely be raised as equity investment. Again, business angels are a possible source of investment particularly if the returns are seen to be high. In some countries, there are specialist investment funds and incubators which invest in start-ups. Another source of finance is corporate investment where there is a strategic fit with the start-up. In such cases, innovation or niche expertise in the start-up is invested in by a larger company who would prefer not to have to do that work in-house themselves at higher cost. Here the size of the investment can vary significantly. None of these sources of finance are easy to obtain. But you would like more than money. What is preferable is an investor who brings skills, contacts and experience to the business. This is where corporate investment is highly valuable.

What are the chances of raising equity investment for a start-up? Unfortunately, very few start-ups succeed in raising finance, a success rate of below 5% is frequently quoted. Why should this be so? Clearly, the perception that start-ups are very high risk is the dominant factor, but in addition the other most common reasons investors reject proposals are:

- Inexperienced management team—gaps in management skills
- Very early stage—no proof of principle
- Financial forecasts speculative
- Financial returns low
- Products not scalable
- Market understanding weak
- No clear exit route for investors.

But even if you are successful in raising finance, the time required can be long, anything from 3 to 12 months which puts a serious brake on the growth of your start-up. Unfortunately, that is yet another hardship you have to endure.

Of course, before you make any attempt to raise finance you have to decide what you believe your company is worth. This is a key piece of information that an investor would want to enable them to assess the attraction or otherwise of the investment opportunity. We have discussed company valuations before but difficult as it might be, you have to have a figure in mind. Investors will use your valuation to compare the risks and returns of your business opportunity against others so an unreasonably high valuation would deter interest in your company.

If you are successful in interesting some investors it is certain that they will follow up by undertaking a due diligence on you by asking many, many questions about you, your product and your business. This is another reason why writing a plan for your business is important, it means that you will be in a much better position to respond to these questions. The due diligence is most often undertaken by experienced business advisors appointed by the potential investors. Here again the work you've done in planning and documenting your business will be of great benefit during this process. As the company progresses, there will be many further rounds of funding to be raised to take you into product development, pre-production, production and launch, etc. At each of these stages further questions arise and decisions have to be made. Here again, a well-written business plan should enable you to address these questions and make the right decisions.

Reference

[1] Moon J 2007 *How to Make and Impact: Influence, Inform and Impress with your Reports, Presentations and Business Documents* (Harlow: Financial Times/Prentice Hall)

Chapter 9

Managing a start-up

When you start a company, as the founder, you'll no doubt want to do as much as possible yourself to keep costs down. But sooner or later this will no longer be possible and you'll be forced to recruit others who will manage the areas of business that lie outside your range of skills. In putting together such a management team, what is required is to match jobs with people's skills and, very importantly, to hire only the best people available. Resist the temptation to appoint family, friends, or others because of their likeable personalities.

Managing a tech start-up, usually with limited financial resources, can be a daunting task. A start-up commonly exists in an environment of fast-changing technology so that constant vigilance is needed by the management team to steer the company to eventual success. There is also the fear of running out of money in most start-ups. This is, after all, often the reason why a business fails, so it is crucial that someone with financial expertise and experience in raising money is part of the management team early in the life of the company.

Many start-ups fail and about half don't survive beyond five years. There are many reasons for this so let's look at what management can do to improve the chances of success.

The founder

In the early days of a business start-up it is most often the case that the inventor is the founder of the company, the driving force who decides the business strategy of the company. It is also not at all unusual for the founder to passionately believe that the invention is the unique and prized asset of the company. However, and most often to the surprise and disappointment of the founder, investors are more likely to support a company if they have confidence in the management team rather than the innovative business idea or invention. This can be hard to accept, particularly for those scientists from backgrounds in academia and business where creative ideas are highly recognised. Founders have to be realistic about their strengths and

doi:10.1088/978-0-7503-1146-5ch9

weaknesses so that they can clearly appreciate the need to work with others within a management team. This requires that the founder accepts that for the benefit of the company the leading executive role, the managing director (chief executive officer) be an entrepreneur with a track record of commercial success. This is a realisation which often only occurs later in the life of a start-up when circumstances such as running out of money, confused product development or lack of market identi-fication force a change at the top of the company. Avoid making this mistake, it can be a costly one.

Recruiting

You certainly want the best management team that you can find. Finding good executives is not easy but you know that it is their skills that will determine the success or otherwise of the company. So how do you find good staff?

Perhaps the best way is through executive search firms. This is an expensive way to go but given the importance of having the right people there is probably no real alternative. The advantage is that the candidates they find for you are screened to match your requirements. These may also be candidates that you would not have been able to locate by any other means. Classified advertisements in newspapers or even bulletin boards on the internet are unlikely to provide you with the calibre of person you are looking for.

It may also be that during your time in research you've come across contacts with the appropriate business experience to join your team, if not for the long term then at least during the early start-up period of the company. But make sure that you subject the contact to the same scrutiny as you would anyone else. Be wary of hiring friends. They will assume that they have the right skill levels for the job which could later lead to disagreements about work in the company and leave your friendship in ruins.

Remember also the advice in chapter 5 from Gareth Williams: 'A successful start-up is also about culture—the way the entrepreneur behaves will ripple down within the company'.

When you hired executives to your management team it was because you trusted that their judgement would be better than yours in their particular area of responsibility. When you disagree, the chances are that you're wrong and they're right. Decide early in the life of the company how you will deal with such conflicts because for certain they will happen. Otherwise, if you agree on everything with any of them, one of you is redundant!

The management team

It is generally agreed among business advisors and investors that a talented management team is of utmost importance for the success of a start-up. Scientists entering the business world will find that investors don't generally rate original ideas that highly. It is a common belief in business that a brilliant idea with poor management is less likely to succeed than a moderately good idea with excellent management. What is important is not so much the innovative idea but its implementation by the management team. Another example of this is the case of entrepreneurs who have taken an idea that has been known for years, made small changes to it and on this basis formed a company and driven it to success. So it's more implementation than innovation that counts.

What is also crucial is the appreciation that no matter what the idea, there must be a need for the product—you need customers. It is unfortunately the case that many start-ups fail because of the hopeful assumption that there would be a demand for the product—the belief that 'they will beat a path to our door'. No, they won't. The identification of the potential customers for your business is a task that an experienced management team will undertake with much greater scrutiny than the initial survey that you, as founder, would have done to test the viability of the business.

Money

Start-ups fail because they run out of money so finance is a key issue and should be effectively addressed even as early as the research stage of the company's life. Often the creative scientist, the founder, is not financially minded so that it is essential to include someone in the management team who is, and particularly someone who is familiar with raising money.

The market

The way in which a start-up identifies and addresses its market is a key to its success. A thorough understanding of the resources and time that are required to develop the route to market is also essential. Many start-ups fail because of a lack of planning in this regard. So, one of the crucial tasks that management has to face is accessing the market. This can take a long time particularly for a start-up with limited resources. This undertaking is often made worse by waiting too long before launching the product. Successful entrepreneurs are often seen to have acted quite differently— they go to market at the earliest possible opportunity and rely on customer feedback to further improve their product.

For an excellent analysis of how to identify your customers, sell to your customers and how to scale up your business, refer to *Disciplined Entrepreneurship* by Bill Aulet [1], a book that will benefit any start-up managerial team.

The start-up management team

From day one of a tech start-up it will become clear that planning and implementing the various strategies of the company will require the recruitment of staff. You don't, of course, have to recruit a whole management team from the start, so the question that arises is who should you employ and when. But start-ups usually have limited financial resources so hiring only the right people early on is an important judgement to make.

Consultants

One of the perks of being a scientist involved in research and development is that you are very likely to be in regular contact with experts in your area. These could be collaborators or even friends who may well be willing to give you advice. It would be a good idea to ask these people to be consultants to your company. It may well be the case that at the early stage in the life of your company they would be quite willing to act as consultants without needing payment.

Board of advisors

As we have said before, many founders of tech start-ups are scientists with little or no experience of business. So, a prudent early action is to surround yourself with experienced advisors who have a track record in your business area. They will have skills you lack, make connections for you that could benefit your business, and guide you against making early costly mistakes. These advisors could form your Advisory Board who would meet, say, every six months to help you develop the business. And very importantly, all the advisors would probably agree to be unpaid but be willing to offer their services because of their belief in your product and their interest in seeing the start-up grow. It could also be that they had in mind an equity stake in the company at a later date! Nevertheless, their contribution at an early stage of the company's development could be invaluable to an inexperienced founder.

The first appointment that the founder of a start-up should make is that of the Managing Director (Chief Executive Officer).

Managing Director

The Managing Director (MD) is responsible for everything in the company and is everyone's boss. A key skill required of the MD is to be able to decide the strategy of the company and guide it successfully through future competitive market conditions. An MD is expected to have the skill to hire the best management team but also be decisive enough to fire those who don't perform.

A founder of a tech start-up, usually the inventor, with no business experience would be well advised to hand over the running of the company to a successful entrepreneur. This is a painful realisation for a founder who not uncommonly believes that he/she has coped with much more difficult problems. Yes, but probably not problems that need addressing armed only with incomplete or uncertain information as is the lot of the entrepreneur who has to make business decisions based on a high element of uncertainty and risk. Risk-taking is not in the nature of scientists but is unavoidable in a start-up. This is why a start-up should be managed by a business manager with entrepreneurial skills in the many areas of business of which the taking of calculated risk is part of their skill set and which they most probably find highly motivating.

So the appointment of an MD should be made at the earliest possible opportunity. In a tech start-up this could be at the time that proof of principle of the intellectual property, usually the invention, has been confirmed. The MD would not only manage the day-to-day running of the company but would undertake the raising of funds for the company.

An entrepreneurial MD will, of course, not be cheap and for a start-up this could be a problem. Further, investors would almost certainly expect their investment to be used directly in developing the business of the company rather than on high salaries. An option would be to offer the MD an equity stake in the company and a smaller salary, an arrangement that potential investors would most likely accept. Acceptance by the MD of such an arrangement would also indicate a degree of confidence in the future success of the start-up.

Finance Director/Accounts Manager

Finance managers aren't the favourites in companies—they stop you buying the latest equipment or facilities that would be 'nice to have' but will spend money instead on boring things like paying off loans. But the Finance Director will also direct the attention of the MD and the Sales Director to the customers and products where it is necessary to concentrate the company's effort so as to maximise profits.

Your Finance Director handles the money, determines the financial strategies and creates the company budgets, tasks that scientists don't commonly have much familiarity with or indeed find at all interesting.

At an early state a start-up will not need a Finance Director. That is an appointment that can be left to when the start-up begins to trade, sales have been achieved and are increasing. In the meantime—at least in the early life of the company—the general management of the company's account can be done by an Accounts Manager, even part-time.

Marketing Director

The success of a business relies heavily on the skill of the Marketing Director who is responsible for the marketing and sales strategy of the company and for its implementation. The Marketing Director will have the experience and skill to get to know your business sector well and so position your product appropriately and differentiate it from competitor products. The Marketing Director will also be responsible for getting distributors for the company (if appropriate) and to create a need for the product in the market place.

The appointment of a Marketing Director should be made in the early life of the start-up when the development stages of the technology have been completed and the emergence of a product is certain. At this stage the launch and sales of the product could be one or two years away.

Sales staff

It would be a good idea to take on sales staff well before the launch of the product to allow time for training. The decision to appoint would be made by the MD after consultation with the Marketing Director.

Chief Technology Officer or R&D Director

In a tech start-up the founder of the company is usually the inventor. As we have said before, a founder who is smart enough to recognise that they don't have the skills and personality or even an interest in running a company will seek out a successful entrepreneur to act as MD (CEO). To appoint someone else to be your boss in your own company, for many, may not be easy! The most appropriate position for the founder or inventor, to take is Chief Technology Officer or Research and Development Director—a title that might be easier to accept. The R&D Director would, of course, be responsible for developing the invention to product stage, stay aware of technology developments that could impact the company's products and, when necessary, undertake further research and development to stay ahead of the competition.

Patent Lawyer and Accountant

The start-up must, at its initiation, appoint an accountant to deal with the company registration and filing of annual company financial information to the tax authorities in the relevant country, among other legal requirements that a company must fulfil. The outlay here is most commonly a fee for preparing the company's annual return to the tax authorities.

Board of Directors

As the company develops there will be a time when your group of advisors could more formally become the Board of Directors. These directors could continue as advisors as before or be given certain responsibilities in the company. A board of directors could bring expertise that you would not have in the management team such as law, contacts with investors, regulatory matters and generally in business strategy. A further advantage is that members of the board may well be willing to accept a low annual fee.

Reference

[1] Aulet B 2013 *Disciplined Entrepreneurship: 24 Steps to a Successful Startup* (Hoboken, NJ: Wiley)

Chapter 10

In conclusion

Start-ups are a journey into uncertainty and entrepreneurs are individuals who are comfortable with uncertainty, thrive on challenges and are prepared to take risks. Unfortunately, most start-ups fail as we have stated earlier in this book. So, let's review why some start-ups succeed and others fail. Ultimately, a business fails because it runs out of money. As we have discussed in different chapters in this book there are many reasons why this can happen. Weakness in the management team, lack of customers, wrong business model, inability to raise funds and the ability of the entrepreneur are all factors that contribute to the failure of a start-up. Let's then summarise the dos and don'ts for a start-up just as a reminder.

Firstly, the founding entrepreneur is the driving force of the start-up but should realise early on that it is critical to create a team to run the business. It is well accepted that investors regard the management team more highly than the idea or invention on which the company is based.

Entrepreneurs may be disappointed to realise that even a brilliant idea is no guarantee of success and is most often not highly rated by investors. It's not invention or innovation that counts—it's implementation. A start-up with a brilliant idea also needs brilliant execution. Even so, a good idea, no matter how well executed will still need to have customers for the eventual products or services. Many start-ups fail because of a lack of demand for their product.

Where a market for the product exists, accessing it takes time and start-ups often don't have the manpower to overcome these challenges. The way the company gains access to its market, its business model requires a thorough understanding of the resources required to get a start-up to eventual profitability. A lack of planning in this regard is often a reason why start-ups fail.

What we have said many times in this book is that ultimately start-ups, like other businesses, fail because they run out of money. This is an issue that needs to be thoroughly researched even at as early as the research stage of the company. If the

doi:10.1088/978-0-7503-1146-5ch10

entrepreneur is not financially savvy then it is necessary to accept this as a weakness and appoint someone in the team who is.

Most start-ups have limited resources so managing finances is crucial. The company needs to identify what its financial requirements are to achieve its milestones and become skilled at meeting these objectives even with these financial limitations. Doing more with less should be the order of every day. Start-ups need to manage their finances efficiently and avoid unnecessary expenses. Expenditure on travel can be a particular culprit—there is the tendency to confuse motion with progress. You should expect your CEO to run things on a lean budget.

Many start-ups fail but the ones that survive are run by entrepreneurs who generally have certain qualities. We've discussed these before but let's remind ourselves about these characteristics.

As we have emphasised before, a start-up needs an outstanding CEO (MD) to whom the founder would have to report—a necessity that often requires tactful persuasion! Such a CEO will have well-honed networking skills and have influential contacts who can gain the start-up access to investors and partners. Further, the CEO will have the ability to guide the founding management team through the inevitable difficult times and inspire the team to make whatever sacrifices are necessary, be they in time demands, salary cuts or bonuses, to make the start-up successful.

Time and speed are of the essence in the running of a start-up. Successful start-ups get things done on time and put in whatever time is required to outpace their competitors. An experienced management team knows this and will strive to reach their goals as quickly as possible. Also, speed helps because the faster you can make your inevitable mistakes and learn from them the better!

We have stated many times in this book that entrepreneurs and their team should have well-researched information about their customers and have a clear route to market. Some start-ups create products that are ahead of their time so that identifying customers will take much longer than for products that are 'no-brainers'. In this case you will need tenacity to stick to your belief that you'll be proved right in the end and that the market will in time emerge—a very courageous decision to have to make. Nevertheless, determination and persistence are key components of success in any start-up. It's worth constantly reminding yourself that your start-up ultimately has to make money, it has to be profitable to survive. That is its objective. It is not a hobby.

Starting a company can be challenging and stressful and certainly is risky but make it a calculated risk. What I've found helpful in starting a company, and I've done this a few times, is to anticipate what failure might look like. If you can live with that then you should feel a little more confident about starting your company.

Appendix

Example company business plan format for fundraising after start-up

Executive summary A-1
The team A-3
Business overview A-4
Market A-5
Strategic Analysis A-9
Competitive advantage A-10
The product A-11
Operations A-12
Sales and marketing A-14
Financials A-17
Exit strategy A-18
Appendix A-18

Executive summary

The ### phone case controller brings break-through NFC harvesting technology to the masses for a better gaming experience integrated into a slim and appealing phone case. As smartphones become bigger and more powerful, so have the games that are being played on them. With phone manufacturers continuously pushing towards sleeker designs with fewer physical buttons, the games have had to evolve into utilizing the touch screen as the main control input. Although touchscreens have greatly improved the interface with our devices, phone developers have yet to generate real tactile feedback for the user. With the addition of pressure sensitive physical buttons and twin joysticks integrated into the phone case, this opens up new possibilities for game developers to create more immersive games.

The market for smartphones has grown tremendously in the last five years globally and, in turn, so has the mobile gaming market. Reports state that over 50% of smartphone users will play at least one game on their phone, over a wide range of demographics.

In this growing market, *** has developed ### a smartphone case with integrated pressure sensitive controls that require no external power for a better gaming experience. The technology is a recent breakthrough and uses a chip to communicate and harvest power through the phone's NFC function. *** have submitted a patent application for this technology. As ### gains traction, the long-term plan is for ### to create a gaming cloud platform where players can play anywhere whilst saving space on the phone for photos and videos.

Strategic analysis reveals that with a strong international team with diverse backgrounds, *** will be able to take advantage of the lack of competition in the market if the company moves quickly, becoming the first-mover in this product. Further competitive advantage lies in the board's diverse access to manufacturers in Asia, giving *** the ability to negotiate better invoicing agreements, MOQs, and supplier sourcing.

*** has developed a working prototype for two android phones and is now ready for production. An iPhone version is in development and the next generation of smartphones is already being considered.

Suppliers, manufacturing, and assembly will be sourced from Asia. Only three companies in the world are known to be able to supply the unique NFC chip and *** has made an agreement with one of these in Thailand. The final assembly and warehouse will be located in China where the newly appointed director *yyy* will use his network and cultural understanding.

has already experienced some success with PR not only in the UK, but also in the US, Japan and China. There are more than 75 articles praising the product in at least three different languages. *** will use this momentum to drive further digital marketing for online sales and create meaningful partnerships for wholesale deals.

The company is looking to grow exponentially in the next five years with global sales to hit £x million per quarter on the sales of the phone cases alone. With £x invested into *** in 2016, the current valuation of the company is £x.

An exit is expected after year five by acquisition from a large game developer with a 5-10x multiplier. Possible buyers would include but are not limited to Nintendo, Sega, Sony, and Google.

The Team

Nice photograph here.	**Name, position...** has a PhD in mobile telecommunications and electronic engineering. Before that he worked at ——————— as an engineer. He is responsible for day-to-day business activities as well as leading the technical team.
Nice photograph here.	**Name, position...** studied in —, — and has a PhD in —. She previously worked for ———. She is responsible for social media activities and company internal affairs.
Nice photograph here.	**Name, job title....** has been a business strategist for over 16 years with extensive experience taking brands to market across multiple sectors. She is helping the company in various aspects of business development, including strategy planning, growth hacking, and branding.
Nice photograph here.	**Name, job title**, studied in —, has a degree in — from —. He has family relations with Chinese producers and distributors, as well as middle east distributors. He will be helping the company in manufacturing and selling in China/Middle East, including advertising, selling strategy, planning, branding, and manufacturing.

Consultants/Advisers

Nice photograph here.	**Name, job title**, consultant's own description of themselves.
Nice photograph here.	**Name, job title,** consultant's own description of themselves.

Business Overview

Vision
To be the controller of choice for mobile games and remote control devices

Purpose
To create an integrated ecosystem for gamers by providing a better gaming experience through both hardware and software solutions.

The problem
As phones become more and more powerful, the quality of games in terms of graphics, storylines, gameplay and social interactions has increased exponentially. As the trend of phone design from phone manufacturers continues towards the minimalist philosophy, the one aspect of gaming that is difficult to innovate is the controls.

The solution
Product
is, in its most basic form, a phone case that sits on your device. But with dual analogue controller sticks and pressure sensitive shoulder buttons it also turns your smartphone into a gaming powerhouse. This offers the user an enhanced gaming experience closer to home-based gaming consoles, and also protects the phone.

Brand

In addition to the ### game controller, *** is developing a subscription-based cloud gaming service that enables users to play PC and Console games in addition to Mobile games on multiple devices, including Smartphones and Smart TVs.

This prevents the user having to purchase and download multiple games for use across different platforms. In other words, the user will only have to pay once (pay-monthly subscription or pay-as-play) for one device, one experience, one game, one cloud!

All games accessed through the ### app are optimised to work using the ### game controller, which enhances mobile gaming experience.

A full working prototype of the cloud gaming service is available and will be launched once the required number of game publishers have signed up to the service.

The business model, legal structure and ownership

There are two main sources of revenue for ***. The company will initially start trading by designing, prototyping, and releasing our patented phone case for sale, targeting the major global markets of UK, China, India, Japan, and the US. This will be achieved by both B2B and B2C channels partnering with network operators, phone resellers, and online retail initially.

The second source of revenue will come from a subscription sale model for a cloud-based gaming platform that *** plans to release once the first three models of phone cases have begun.

The company will be in a unique situation, joining only a handful of companies that sell both hardware and software.

is the trading name held by and 100% owned by the company *** Ltd.

Market

Size—growing market

The market for smartphones has been growing at an incredible rate in the last 10 years. Since the introduction of the iPhone 3 from Apple, communication has been revolutionized for the consumer. Although the penetration rate is higher in the US, China and India have seen the greatest growth (>10% in the previous five years) and active users (> 1 bn handsets connected).

There are currently 2.08 bn smartphone users (taking into account users with multiple connections) globally with an expected rise to 2.3 bn handsets by the end of 2017 (statista, 2016). Studies show that globally, over 50% of smartphone users will play games on their handset, giving *** a potential market of over 1 bn users in a market worth £19 bn (superdataresearch, 2016).

Global Smartphone users forecast 2014–2019

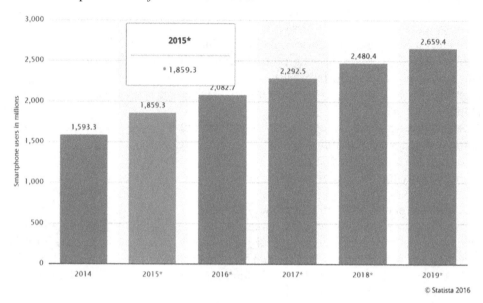

© Statista 2016

Analysis of the most downloaded games for android in 2016, show that the top 10 game downloads (androidpit, 2016) averaged 180 million downloads per game with over 500 million downloads each for the top 26. Out of these, 10 were not only compatible with ###, but ### would have improved the gaming experience.

Demography
Research shows a large target market for ###, but the core customers will be gamers who have a strong interest in improved gaming control and feedback. Studies have shown that of the 20 million gamers in the UK, the median age is 31 years old of, which 52% are female. This ratio changes to 48% for the 198 million users in the US.

The market in Asia can be broken down to the 'big three' which includes China, Japan, and South Korea, with a combined revenue of £10.5 bn. Surprisingly China, even with a larger user base, falls behind Japan in terms of total revenue in mobile gaming.

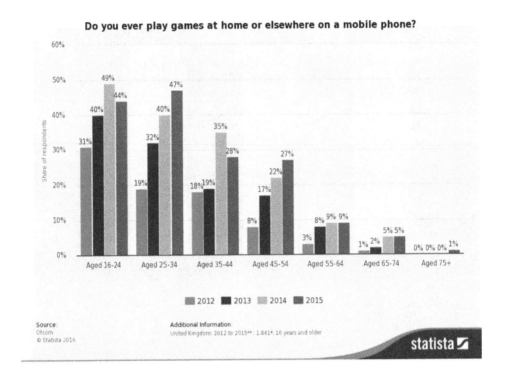

Do you ever play games at home or elsewhere on a mobile phone?

Competition

Direct competition

There are currently no gaming controls integrated into a phone case like ### on the market. The company considers this product the first of its kind for the reasons listed in the product section. There are two things that make ### truly unique, first of all it is the only controller that uses NFC technology which negates the need for batteries, and secondly it fits over the phone without creating bulk or weight.

INSERT A BEAUTIFUL, PROFESSIONALLY PRODUCED IMAGE OF YOUR PRODUCT HERE

Indirect competition

There are a number of indirect competitors on the market and due to be available on the market soon. Of the top 10 controllers readily available on the market today, only one does not require an external battery source. All other competitors use Bluetooth to connect to the device and require a separate battery source. The competitors include:

– Phonejoy	Bluetooth, bulky, battery required
– Moga	Bluetooth, sep device, AAA batteries
– Icade 8bitty	Bluetooth, AAA batteries
– 60beat	Wired 3.5 mm headphone jack
– impulse (keychain)	
– Steelseries Free	Bluetooth, built-in battery
– idroid	Bluetooth, built-in battery
– zeemote	Bluetooth
– nykyo playpad	Bluetooth, built-in battery
– icontrol pad 2	Bluetooth, built-in battery

Other competition

Other handheld consoles that are solely built for the purposes of gaming can be considered as competition for ###. These devices range in price from £67 to £414 and generally have a wide variety of well-developed game titles. These include:

– Nintendo 3DS XL	– £139
– Sony playstation Vita	– £134
– Nvidia Shield	– £414
– Nintendo 2DS	– £67
– Nintendo 3DS	– £135

Strategic Analysis

SWOT analysis

The most important internal conditions for the company	
Internal Strengths	**Internal Weaknesses**
Strong team of founders with a mix of experience, skills, qualifications, and experience.	Brand new product could have teething issues
	Expensive R&D
Product prototype, tested and ready for production	
	Expensive to re-tool each new android phone that comes out
Patent Pending	
No direct competitors that can seamlessly integrate external gaming controls	
External Opportunities	**External Threats**
With the development of Android NFC, Apple case is easy to implement	Apple has locked NFC features to payment only for iPhones and may never open up NFC for this use
First mover advantage	
	Competition from gaming companies like Nintendo, Sony, or Microsoft
Access to markets with the fastest growing adoption rate of smartphones in the world	Cloud based games service can be replicated very quickly
Fast paced emerging technology will make picking up the concept faster	Technology may not keep up with other developers
Integration with VR gaming and Smartphones	
The most important external conditions for the company	

Risk
   a. The threat from new entrants is considered **low**
      ■ R&D of harvesting NFC to power the case is high
      ■ Tooling and manufacturing cost is high
      ■ Time taken to develop product is long
   b. Threats from substitutes are considered **medium**
      ■ Controllers are within the same price range and have the same function in terms of gaming. There are many similar types of these controllers
      ■ The mobile gaming platforms do not provide a cloud service for integration of games
      ■ Separate consoles spend more in game development with a dedicated platform
   c. Bargaining power of suppliers is considered **medium**
      ■ Suppliers for the NFC chip have more power as they license the product to ***
      ■ Other components can be manufactured by other companies and are interchangeable
   d. Bargaining power of buyers is considered **high**
      ■ Buyer can buy substitutes easily
      ■ Many substitutes to choose from
   e. Rivalry amongst competitors is considered **high**
      ■ No direct competitors as yet with this technology
      ■ With high rates of smartphone adoption, gaming companies and networks will want to be in the market
      ■ Once idea comes on the market, other companies can use different technology to integrate controls into phone case for a similar device

Competitive advantage

Differentiation advantage ### is unique. NFC technology allows ### to be relatively thin compared with the closest competition. The biggest benefit for the consumer is one less device to recharge and carry around to game with. This will appeal to a broader audience.

also gives users access to their cloud gaming network, saving the user space on their devices for photos, music, messages, and videos instead.

First mover advantage We anticipate there could be a company aiming to be the fast second, and expect a conservative estimate of at least six months development for the competitor. Development for ### at *** required 18 months to be production ready.

Strategic summary
The results show a strong case for taking ### into the market. The company must move quickly in order to take full advantage of being the first to market, thus capturing the audience and establishing itself as 'the' smartphone gaming solution.

The analysis further reveals the greatest strength of the company is derived from the diverse team members with a mix of gaming, technological, process management, and networks in the industry. With the product now mostly developed, the focus now lies on manufacturing and supply chain.

Although start-ups will find it difficult to enter and compete with ***, more established game developers producing hardware or with plans to enter the market could move faster with access to more funds and talent.

The overall strategy of the business is aimed at ### becoming the number one game controller across all mobile devices. In addition to this, through its subscription-based gaming service, ### aims to onboard mainstream game and indie game developers offering their games through the ### cloud platform.

In achieving this strategy ### intends to invest in a number of key areas including:

- Sales and marketing
- Partnership activation
- Product development.

In the short term ### plans to build a relationship with 1–2 partners and to increase growth and scale through extending geographic regions with existing partners and then adding additional partners in Y2 and Y3.

Currently ### is in negotiation with Japan, Chinese and Middle East companies regarding exclusive distribution licences. Such licences will require its distributors to sell x units of ### in a six month period to obtain its exclusive licence.

The product

Attributes

A full working prototype of the game controller is available for demonstration purposes.

In developing ### there were multiple considerations and expectations from the founders. The phone case first of all had to be functional as a phone case, which meant

- It is slim and protects your phone like a case (dual purpose)
- It is easy to fit on to the phone and is lightweight (Snap-On-Snap-Off)
- It is aesthetically appealing.

To make it a ### phone case, two more factors were added as attributes, the case is also used:

- To provide users with an enhanced gaming experience whilst on the move; and
- To provide users with a modern carry less, care free experience.

Some of the main advantages of the ### game controller are:
- It enables users to play games using the full screen
- ### controller can connect with other app-controlled devices such as drones, robots, and cars
- It is game-ready.

Some of the differentiators are:
- It is battery-less and never needs to be charged (harvests energy through NFC)
- It is wireless (communicates using NFC).

The game controller has intuitive and responsive shoulder buttons and dual joysticks, bringing the excitement of console gaming to smartphones. The current prototype has been designed to work on NFC-enabled Android smartphones. To increase its appeal, the intention is to develop a working prototype for other phone types that are not NFC enabled.

INSERT PROFESSIONALLY PRODUCED, DETAILED IMAGE OF THE PRODUCT

Technology
- NFC: a unique 60 Hz two-way NFC protocol—*** has cracked energy-harvesting technology and two-way 60 Hz NFC communication. Smartphones with NFC technology will usually send a signal that is more powerful than necessary. This allows ### to harvest the extra energy that is being generated.
- Patent-pending

is currently patent-pending. See documentation in the appendix.

Operations

Product lifecycle
Design
The product design lifecycle will be required for every new model *** plans to bring to the market. Although the technology is ready for production, the design process must be used to implement into new phone cases as phone manufacturers update their range. The design process follows these steps:
1. **Understanding the market** *** must understand the market and its consumers before creating each new case. The new case should have a large enough market to warrant the time and funds that will be spent for development. This will include research into prior models, public opinions and reviews about upcoming models, and forecasting based on previous launches.
2. **Design** Once a model has been selected for production, the design team's job will be to integrate the NFC chip into the new ### case. The design must fit in with the ### design philosophy of being thin, integrated, and battery-less.

3. **Prototype and in-house testing** The phone case, once designed, will be tested for durability and usability. The case must offer similar protection to a case of similar design (without the gaming controls) and the electronics and software must marry up with the phone.

4. **Beta testing and feedback** The feedback loop is used to determine if the product fits in with all the criteria that ### carries. Furthermore, it allows *** to test the product with users and gain feedback on improvements, and whether or not consumers would actually buy the case. If the product does not meet certain requirements or test groups agree that certain features should be added or taken away, the product goes back into stage one and starts the cycle again until management is satisfied that the product is ready for production.

has developed two android phone cases which are now ready for production. The next stage of development will focus on creating an iPhone case. The challenge of this project lies in the 'closed' nature of the iOS, which has locked the NFC capability to payments only.

Future models will be selected by the expected volume of sales to maximize the potential market for ###. Current targets for the case include Samsung, Sony, Huawei, and Xiaomi.

Product development
The process contains three main blocks as shown below:

1. **Supplier and manufacturer sampling**
   a. **MOQ** For initial orders, the minimum order quantity will play a large role in cashflow. The lower the MOQ, the better the flexibility of the business.
   b. **Material** There are four main parts that make up the final product including the plastic moulding, circuit board, NFC chip, and sensor. Of these parts, only the NFC is difficult to source as there are only three factories in the world that are able to produce the chips to specification.
   c. **Capacity** A consideration will be the extent to which the supplier or manufacturer is able to handle increasing volume in a short timeframe.
   d. **Cost** The strategy of *** is not to be the cheapest controller on the market, therefore we will not simply be looking for the cheapest manufacturer. Although cost will be a large factor, the ability to deliver as promised, invoicing terms, and MOQ terms will affect the decision in choosing the manufacturer.
   e. **Metrics** *** and the manufacturer should agree on the metric to which the products will be measured for quality control.
   f. **Time** The time-frame in which the factory can deliver the finished product will be a consideration. This will also depend on the wholesale end.

2. **Testing**
   a. **Quality control** This will include measuring metrics determined in the previous step. These will include the thresholds for, but not limited to, faults, correct alignment (fit), and colour.

b. **Durability** Testing will determine how well the case works as just a simple case. Although ### will not make any claims for extreme durability, it should not provide less protection than a simple plastic aftermarket case. The company will test for, but once again not limit to, falls, abrasion resistance, and button fatigue.

3. **Production** There are four main parts to production that involves coordination from at least three different countries. The four major parts are:

   a. **Sensor** This can be sourced from manufacturers in both Taiwan and China. A Chinese manufacturer will likely be chosen for logistic reasons.

   b. **Electronic circuit board** This will be sourced from China where the cost is lower. This manufacturer will receive the NFC chips from Thailand and integrate it into the board.

   c. **NFC chip** Will be sourced from Thailand, one of the three companies in the world with the capability to produce this technology. There is already an agreement in place to supply *** for the next five years.

   d. **Plastic molding** Will be in China again. This manufacturer will also be where the final product is finished.

4. **Distribution** With two main customers, a hybrid push–pull strategy process will be implemented.

   a. **Wholesale** Wholesale customers will primarily pull, allowing *** to manufacture according to order. The most important aspect is managing expectations on time. Products will ship from the factory direct to the phone manufacturer or wholesaler

   b. **Retail** A warehouse near the final assembly point will be advantageous with individual orders being sent direct to the customer when the order is placed online. Shipping costs per item is more cost effective from China.

Sales and marketing

Objectives

Marketing

- Brand ### as the gaming controller that everyone should buy.
- Digital marketing to reach a combined 100 000 unique followers through Facebook, Instagram, Linkedin, Pinterest, Youtube, Google+, Twitter, WeChat etc within 12 months of launch.
- Drive traffic to our website and reach 1000 visits per day within 12 months.
- Optimise SEO for ### to appear as top searches for android or iOs gaming

Sales

- Sales targets set for from launch
  - o   6 months 100k units
  - o 12 months 350k units
  - o 18 months 550k units

Product

The target audience for ### includes:

- Casual and hardcore gamers on the move (penetration of 48% or 580 m gamers with 19% CAGR 2014–2018).
- Owners and buyers of app connected devices
- Virtual reality (VR) gamers

Even though ### carries multiple benefits when compared to indirect competitors, the main benefit for hardcore gamers will be the increased control (pressure sensitive controls) and more screen space (fingers can be kept free from the screen).

Casual gamers will see the gaming controls as a value add to a protective phone case they would have bought anyway.

Key Messages:

The competitor profiles show that the product range of ###'s direct competitors is

a) Based on one type of technology (Bluetooth)
b) Separate console requiring separate batteries.

will base promotional activities on the following key messages:

I. More control in-game
II. Unobstructed screen during game-play
III. Protective case
IV. No battery required.

Continuous additional key messages will be formulated based on feedback after launch.

Place

1. Online advertising:

Matching the primary distribution channels (ecommerce and wholesale), ### will heavily focus on online advertising to raise brand awareness and generate website traffic to drive sales. This includes:

I. Web/display banners on websites, blogs and online communities/forums relevant to our target groups, including the following categories:
    a) Gaming sites (IGN, Kokatu, Polygon, Gamespot etc)
    b) New tech websites (Gizmag, Gizmodo etc)
II. E-mail advertising (using 3rd party provider with access to large database; recipient list tailored to ###'s target groups)
III. Pre-targeting: display online ads based on previous activities
IV. Post- and pre-roll ads on YouTube
V. Search engine marketing (SEM)—keyword based advertisement
    a) Android games
    b) Android controller
    c) Gaming phone case
    d) Phone case contoller

e) Others (depending on in-depth keyword research)
VI. Search engine optimisation (SEO) to improve Google search ranking
VII. Mobile advertising including in-game advertising
VIII. Facebook advertising (CPC display banners, Facebook email targeting).

2. Social media

Almost all smartphone users are familiar with social media and companies are using social media for commercial purposes. Consumers use it to follow their favourite brands, access special offers and make purchases. Complementing online advertising as well as PR activities (see below), ### will make extensive use of multiple social media channels to share multimedia content, communicate key messages, interact with existing and potential customers, and generate website traffic. In phase 2, local social media channels will be created for each country.

Facebook
- Share company news
- Receive customer feedback
- Promote new products and product lines
- Share multimedia content (new images and videos)
- Host competitions

Youtube/Vimeo
- Product videos
- Instructional videos
- Image videos
- Event videos (### exhibits)

Pinterest
- Product images
- Event images
- Instructional infographics

Instagram
- Product images
- Event images (e.g. product shoots etc)

Twitter
- Share company news
- Receive customer feedback
- Promote new products and product lines
- Share multimedia content (new images and videos)
- Identify new customers
- Customer research.

Publicity/public relations

has already had a significant amount of success in PR. There are currently x articles (see appendix) introducing ### with positive reviews. To further support marketing and advertising activities, we will roll-out new PR campaigns, tailored to the respective markets. Activities will include:

Partnerships

Launch campaign—gaming competition

- Partner with one or multiple game producers/drone manufacturers
    a) Create competitions with game play or drone controls using ###.

Media outreach

I. Send press kits to journalists and bloggers (key media and blogs to be identified)
II. Arrange interviews with ### founders
III. Send sample products for testers.

Testimonials

Identify influencers who will give more coverage of ###.

Promotion

Stimulate initial purchases and drive sales:

- Price promotions (e.g. 'early bird' specials)
- Discounts (packaged into new phone sales for specific models).

Price

As there are no direct competitors to ###, the company is only bound by the price-similar products (indirect competitors). The average price for the external Bluetooth controllers is $x. At the retail level, ### plans to sell for £x (roughly $x). This price reflects great value without giving the impression that the product is 'cheap'.

Competitor pricing	
– Phonejoy	– $x
– Moga	– $x
– Icade 8bitty	– $x
– 60beat wired	– $x
– impulse (keychain)	– $x
– Steelseries Free	– $x
– idroid	– $x
– zeemote	– $x
– icontrol pad 2	– $x

Financials

Funding

*** has received two rounds of funding totaling £x. These were granted for research, enabling the internet of sensors and interactive sensing surface. The founders have also invested £x for research and prototyping. Details of grants can be found in the appendix.

Profit & Loss Statement

See the financials information in chapter 7

Global Sales Targets

Designs & Product Costing

Valuation

Exit strategy

The target return for an early stage technology opportunity is usually in the 5–10x range. Unlike single product technology propositions that rely on driving adoption and subscription revenue, ### is a Hardware AS A Service (HAAS) based proposition where hardware (the controller) will work like a Trojan horse for the subscription-based cloud-gaming service. By introducing all aspects of the business model and accelerating international expansion, the exit value could be substantially higher.

Potential candidates to acquire the business are:

- Leaders in gaming
- Original equipment manufacturers
- Accessory and service providers
- Smart toy companies.

The Company, its management and its advisers make no representation or warranty, expressed or implied, as to the accuracy or completeness of the information either contained in this document (or any appendices) or within any written, electronic or oral communications transmitted in the course of your investigation and evaluation of the business, and will not accept any liability for the accuracy and completeness of such information.

Only specific representations and warranties made to an investor in a definitive executed legal agreement (and subject to any limitations and restrictions as may be specified therein) will have any legal or binding effect.

Appendix

Marketing references
PR Contacts
Grants

9 780750 311472